Steirische Verlagsgesellschaft

GRAZ

The World Heritage

Weltkulturerbe

The Historic Center of Graz | Die Altstadt von Graz

REPUBLIK ÖSTERREICH

Weltkulturerbe | The World Heritage

Dokumentation über die Nominierung der Altstadt von Graz
    Documentation for the nomination of Graz – historic center

Die vorliegende Publikation basiert auf verschiedenen vom Bundesdenkmalamt
und der Stadt Graz zusammengestellten Beiträgen.
    The present study is based on various contributions compiled by the Bundesdenkmalamt and the city of Graz.

Herausgeber: Stadt Graz – Stadtrat Helmut Strobl
    Publisher: The city of Graz; councillor Helmut Strobl

Dokumentation: Amt für Stadtentwicklung und Stadterhaltung: Hansjörg Luser, Astrid M. Wentner
    Documentation: Office for City development and preservation, Hansjörg Luser, Astrid M. Wentner

Grafische Gestaltung: die ORGANISATION, Graz
    Graphic design: die ORGANISATION, Graz

Fotos: Visionas (Andreas Scheucher), Sammlung Karl A. Kubinzky, Foto Langhans, Paul Ott
    Photos: Visionas (Andreas Scheucher), Collection Karl A. Kubinzky, Foto Langhans, Paul Ott

Lithos: Reproteam Graz
    Lithos: Reproteam Graz

Druck: LeykamDruck Graz, gedruckt auf Magnomatt 150 g
    Printing: LeykamDruck Graz, printed on Magnomatt 150 g

Verlag: Steirische Verlagsgesellschaft
    Publisher: Steirische Verlagsgesellschaft

© Graz 2000
ISBN: 3-85489-031-1

Contents

Inhaltsverzeichnis

page | Seite

I. Foreword by the Publisher: the City of Graz | Vorwort des Herausgebers: Stadt Graz   6

II. The Preservation of Mankind's Heritage –   8
An International Collective Task: Bernd von Droste
Die Erhaltung des Erbes der Menschheit –
Eine internationale Gemeinschaftsaufgabe: Bernd von Droste

III. City Profile of Graz | Stadtportrait Graz   15
     Reasons for the Inscription of the Historic Center of Graz on the World Heritage List   26
     Begründung für die Aufnahme der Altstadt von Graz in die World Heritage List

IV. Description of the Historic Center of Graz | Beschreibung der Altstadt von Graz   33
     Historical Development | Geschichtliche Entwicklung   34
     The Urban Development of Graz | Städtebauliche Entwicklung   53
     The Main Buildings of the Historic Center | Die bedeutendsten Bauwerke der Altstadt   75
         Stadtkrone | Die Stadtkrone
         Burg | Die Burg-Anlage
         The Seminary | Das Priesterseminar
         The Old Jesuit University | Die alte Jesuitenuniversität
         The Cathedral | Der Grazer Dom
         The Mausoleum | Das Mausoleum

V. The Application of the City of Graz | Die Bewerbung der Stadt Graz   93
     The UNESCO Convention | Die UNESCO-Konvention   94
     Application Principles | Bewerbungsgrundlagen   97
     Evaluation | Evaluierung   105
     Listing | Die Ernennung   106

VI. Appendix | Anhang   107
     Index of World Heritage | Liste der Weltkulturerbestätten   108
     Literature | Literaturhinweise   118

Foreword by the Publisher: the City of Graz

Vorwort des Herausgebers: Stadt Graz

Das World Heritage Committee beschloss in seiner Sitzung am 1. Dezember 1999 in Marrakesch die Aufnahme der Grazer Altstadt in die Liste der von der UNESCO anerkannten Weltkulturerbestätten. Dieser Akt bestätigt für Graz nicht nur die weltweite Anerkennung der kulturhistorischen Bedeutung seiner Altstadt, sondern dokumentiert auch deren Stellung als schützenswertes Kulturdenkmal höchsten Ranges.

Diese Aufnahme bildet nun den Höhepunkt einer langen Folge von Bemühungen vieler Kräfte: allen voran jenen der Grazerinnen und Grazer, aber auch einer Reihe öffentlicher und privater Institutionen, der zuständigen Fachbeamtenschaft und der verantwortlichen Gestalter der Politik.

Sucht man nach den Wurzeln und Ursachen des bemerkenswert authentischen Erhaltungszustandes der Grazer Altstadt und der allgemeinen Wertschätzung, die sie in der Grazer Bevölkerung genießt, so stößt man zu allererst auf die Medienaktion „Rettet die Grazer Altstadt", die von der Kleinen Zeitung mit ihrem unermüdlichen Altstadtaktivisten Max Mayr ins Leben gerufen wurde. Ihr gelang es, den Abbruch einer wertvollen Häusergruppe und deren Ersatz durch zeitgeistig orientierte Büro- und Geschäftsbauten zu verhindern. Mit diesem Erfolg rückte die gesamte Altstadt immer stärker in den Mittelpunkt des öffentlichen Interesses, das in logischer Folge im Jahre 1974 zum Beschluss des Grazer Altstadterhaltungsgesetzes durch den Steirischen Landtag führte. Dieses Gesetz bildet seither vor allem durch seine enge Verschränkung mit dem Baurecht, dem engagierten Wirken der Altstadtsachverständigenkommission und einer fruchtbaren Kooperation mit dem Bundesdenkmalamt das wirksamste Instrument zum Schutze der Grazer Altstadt.

At its meeting on December 1, 1999 in Marrakech, the World Heritage Committee agreed to inscribe the historic city of Graz on the list of world cultural heritage sites recognized by UNESCO. This act not only confirmed worldwide recognition of the cultural-historical importance of the historic center of Graz, but also formally documented its position as a cultural monument of the highest degree, worthy of protection.

This listing is the culmination of years of endeavor on the part of many. Mainly those of the people of Graz, but also those of a series of public and private institutions, responsible authorities and political decision-makers.

If one is searching for a key to the origins and reasons behind the remarkably authentic state of the Graz historic center's preservation and the general sense of pride among its citizens, one soon comes across the "Rettet die Grazer Altstadt" ('Save the historic center of Graz') media campaign. This campaign was launched by the Kleine Zeitung newspaper and its tireless activist, Max Mayr. It helped to prevent a valuable complex of buildings from being demolished and replaced with modern commercial and office blocks.

As a result of this one success, the public's attention was drawn to the whole of the historic center; this consequently in 1974 led to the Law for the Preservation of the Old City of Graz being passed by the Styrian Diet. Since then this law, in close connection with construction law, the commitment of the Commission of Specialists for Historic Cities and a fruitful cooperation with the Federal Authority for Monuments, has proved the most effective means of protecting the historic city of Graz.

The Councillor for Cultural Affairs, DI Helmut Strobl, and of course the mayor of Graz him-

Für ihre gebührende Anerkennung als Kulturdenkmal und die Aufnahme in die Liste der Weltkulturerbe setzten sich seit Jahren der Kulturstadtrat der Stadt Graz, Dipl.-Ing. Helmut Strobl und natürlich Bürgermeister Alfred Stingl selbst ein. Unterstützt wurden die Bemühungen vor allem in der Phase des konkreten Ansuchens von einer qualifizierten Beamtenschaft: im zuständigen Bundesministerium für Unterrricht und Kunst, im Bundesdenkmalamt Wien und Graz und in der federführenden Abteilung des Magistrats, dem Amt für Stadtentwicklung und Stadterhaltung. Einen großen Anteil am Erfolg der Bewerbung trägt letztlich deren fundierte fachliche Begründung. Sie wurde – auf der Grundlage der von der Kunsthistorikerin Dr. Wiltraud Resch verfassten Kunsttopografie für den ersten Grazer Stadtbezirk – von Frau Dr. Astrid Wentner erarbeitet.

Das vorliegende Buch dokumentiert nun den formalen Ablauf und den Inhalt der Einreichung nach der von der UNESCO festgelegten Ordnung. Den Schwerpunkt bildet dabei die kunst- und bauhistorische Beschreibung, woraus zusammen mit dem hervorragenden Bildmaterial von Dr. Andreas Scheucher zugleich ein interessantes Buch über die Grazer Altstadt entstanden ist. Weiters findet sich darin das im Einzelnen ausgefüllte Bewerbungsformular und nicht zuletzt auch die Begründung der Aufnahme durch das UNESCO-Komitee. Geringfügige Wiederholungen, die sich aus diesem Aufbau ergeben, mögen mit Nachsicht aufgenommen werden.

self, Alfred Stingl both devoted many years of commitment to achieving appropriate recognition for the city's historic center as a cultural monument, and for its inscription on the World Heritage List.

During the phase of application these efforts were supported by an eminently well-qualified body of officials from the Federal Ministry for Education and Arts, the Federal Authorities for Historical Monuments and the department of municipal cooperation responsible, the Authority for Urban Development and Preservation. The success of the application is to be credited to their well-founded specialist assessment, which has been elaborated by Dr. Astrid Wentner on the basis of the art-topography of the first city district of Graz by the art historian Dr. Wiltraud Resch.

The book is a documentation of the formal procedure and the contents of the application according to the order prescribed by UNESCO. It mainly comprises the art and architectural historical description, which, together with some excellent illustrations by Dr. Andreas Scheucher, create a fascinating account of the historic city of Graz. This is accompanied by the completed application torm and the grounds for the listing by the UNESCO committee.

Allowances should therefore be made for any slight repetitions resulting from this structure of the book.

The Preservation of Mankind's Heritage – An International Collective Task

Die Erhaltung des Erbes der Menschheit – Eine internationale Gemeinschaftsaufgabe

Als Erstes möchte ich meiner Freude über die Anerkennung der Altstadt von Graz als UNESCO Welterbe Ausdruck geben und hierbei Goethe zitieren:
„Manches Herrliche der Welt
Ist in Krieg und Streit zerronnen;
Wer beschützt und erhält,
Hat das schönste Los gewonnen."
Herausragende Zeugnisse der Vergangenheit haben oft ein bewegtes Leben. Die ihnen entgegengebrachte Wertschätzung macht sie begehrt. So geraten sie immer wieder zwischen die Fronten von exzessiver Nutzung auf der einen und Schutz und Erhaltung auf der anderen Seite. Ihr Schicksal aber darf uns nicht gleichgültig sein.
Von den sieben Weltwundern der Antike ist heute nur mehr das älteste zu bestaunen: Die bei Giseh am Westufer des Nils errichteten Pyramiden der Pharaonen Cheops, Chephren und Mykerinos (Menkaure); sie haben rund viereinhalb Jahrtausende überdauert.
Verschollen sind die zwölf Meter hohe, gold- und elfenbeingeschmückte Statue des thronenden Zeus in Olympia, die Phidias, der berühmteste Bildhauer des alten Griechenlands, um 430 vor Christus geschaffen hatte; und der Koloss von Rhodos – dieses mehr als 32 Meter hohe bronzene Standbild des Sonnengottes Helios, 290 vor Christus von Chares von Lindos vollendet, war schon 66 Jahre später umgestürzt. Bis auf die Grundmauern abgetragen sind die sogenannten Hängenden Gärten der Semiramis, einer legendären assyrischen Königin (tatsächlich ließ Nebukadnezar II., der wiederum Jerusalem zerstörte und die Juden ins Exil führte, die bepflanzten Terrassen im 6. vorchristlichen Jahrhundert in Babylon anlegen), desgleichen das Grabmal des Mausolos in Halikarnassos, der diese Stadt im Südwesten Kleinasiens Mitte des 4. vorchristlichen Jahr-

First of all, I would like to express my delight at the recognition of the historic city of Graz as a UNESCO World Heritage site, and on this occasion to quote Goethe:
"Many splendors of the world
Were lost in war and fight;
He who protects and preserves
Has won the greatest prize."
Outstanding sites from the past very often have their own eventful history. The esteem they are accorded makes them popular places to visit. So they are repeatedly caught between excessive use on the one hand, and protection and preservation on the other. We cannot afford to be oblivious to their fate.
Of the seven wonders of the ancient world, only the oldest still remains to be admired today. The pyramids of the Pharaohs Cheops, Chephren and Mycerinos (Menkure), built near Giza on the western banks of the river Nile, have survived more than four-and-a-half thousand years. Among the missing wonders are the 12-meter high statue of the enthroned Zeus in Olympia, adorned with gold and ivory, which was created circa 430 BC by Phidias, the most famous sculptor of ancient Greece; the Colossus of Rhodes – the 32-meter high bronze statue of the sun god Helios, completed in 290 BC by Chares of Lindos, which fell just 66 years later; the "Hanging Gardens of Babylon", attributed to the legendary Queen Samu-ramat and which were torn down to the foundation walls (in reality King Nebuchadnezzar II, who destroyed Jerusalem and forced the Jewish people into exile, had the planted terraces of the "Hanging Gardens" created in the sixth century BC). The same fate befell the Mausoleum of Halicarnassus, the tomb of the Anatolian king Mausolus, who in the fourth century BC fortified this city in the southwest of Asia Minor and bestowed on it its splendor. The famous

hunderts befestigt und prunkvoll ausgestattet hatte. Und gänzlich von der Meeresoberfläche verschwunden ist der Leuchtturm auf der ehemaligen Insel Pharus, der erstmals 279 vor Christus Schiffer nach Alexandria leitete. Den Tempel der Artemis in Ephesos schließlich, für den der lykische König Krösus im 6. vorchristlichen Jahrhundert die meisten Säulen gestiftet hatte, äscherte der nach Ruhm gleich welcher Art süchtige Herostratos 356 vor Christus ein.

Diese Beispiele zeigen, dass die Gefährdung und der verantwortungslose Umgang mit kulturellen Zeugnissen der Vergangenheit durchaus kein Problem unseres Jahrhunderts oder gar unserer Generation ist.

Goethe, dessen Wirkungsstätte Weimar pünktlich zu ihrem 750. Geburtstag auf die Welterbeliste gesetzt wurde, gilt – neben Quatremère de Quincy – als einer der großen Protagonisten der Idee eines Kulturerbes der Menschheit, dessen Schutz allen Völkern obliegt.

Eine klare Formulierung dieser Kulturgüterschutzidee finden wir bereits Ende des 18. Jahrhunderts in der Abhandlung „Über die Restauration von Kunstwerken" von Johann Friedrich Meyer, die 1799 im zweiten Band der Propyläen erschien: „Alle Kunstwerke gehören als solche der gesamten gebildeten Menschheit an, und der Besitz derselben ist mit der Pflicht verbunden, Sorge für ihre Erhaltung zu tragen. Wer diese Pflicht vernachlässigt, wer mittelbar oder unmittelbar zum Schaden oder zum Ruin derselben beiträgt, lädt den Vorwurf der Barbarei auf sich – und die Verachtung aller gebildeten Menschen jetziger oder zukünftiger Zeiten wird seine Strafe sein."

Auch wenn diese Überlegungen natürlich aus der damaligen Zeit heraus verstanden werden müssen, in der man die heute so drin-

lighthouse of the former island of Pharos, which in 279 BC guided seamen to Alexandria for the first time, vanished without trace. The temple of Artemis in Ephesus in which Croesus, King of Lydia had most of the columns erected in the sixth century BC, was burnt down by Herostratus in his pursuit of glory in 356 BC.

These examples show that the threat to, and lack of respect for, cultural testaments to the past are matters of concern which should not be assigned exclusively to our century or even our generation.

Goethe, whose Weimar estate was inscribed on the World Heritage List on the occasion of its 750th birthday, was, alongside Quartenière de Quincy, one of the great protagonists of the idea of a world cultural heritage whose preservation is the duty of all peoples.

A clear expression of this notion of the protection of cultural properties is to be found at the end of the 18th century in an essay entitled "Renovation of works of art" by Johann Friedrich Meyer, which was published in 1799 in the second volume of the Propyläen.

"All works of art belong as such to the whole of educated mankind and ownership of them is tied up with the duty to ensure they are preserved. He who neglects this duty, or who is directly or indirectly responsible for damaging or destroying works of art, will stand accused of barbarism. And their punishment will be the contempt of all educated people in the present and in the future."

Although these reflections should be considered within the context of that period, a time when people did not yet know the pressing problems of the increase in world population and the corresponding economic growth required (or were not aware of them), they are nevertheless valuable and essential remarks. In the 19th century, however, these

II

genden Probleme einer weltweit wachsenden Bevölkerung und der dadurch erforderlichen wirtschaftlichen Entwicklung noch nicht kannte (oder zumindest nicht wahrnahm), sind diese Gedankengänge dennoch notwendig und wertvoll. Sie wurden jedoch im 19. Jahrhundert völkerrechtlich nicht umgesetzt. Erst in unserem Jahrhundert wurde ein internationales Rechtsinstrumentarium für den Kulturgüterschutz geschaffen, nachdem der unvergleichlich hohe Verlust an schönsten und bedeutendsten Kultur- und Naturgütern in unserer angeblich so zivilisierten Welt die Allgemeinheit alarmiert hat.

Die bedenkliche Lage von so Unersetzlichem und Lebensnotwendigem wie z. B. die Vielfalt der Arten, und die Gefährdung der für die kreative Entfaltung notwendigen kulturellen Diversität führten schließlich zu neuen Konzepten und zu erstem – wenn auch zaghaftem – internationalem Handeln.

So war die Annahme der Welterbekonvention durch die UNESCO (1972) das logische Ergebnis der erfolgreichen und bis dahin einzigartigen internationalen Kampagne zur Rettung der Tempelanlage von Abu Simbel in Oberägypten, die in den Fluten eines neu errichteten Staudamms zu versinken drohte und nur durch eine kostspielige Umsetzung gerettet werden konnte.

Hier zeigte sich erstmals, dass die internationale Gemeinschaft gewillt war, ein gemeinsames Erbe anzuerkennen und die für dessen Schutz notwendigen Mittel aufzubringen. Der Erfolg der Rettung der Tempelanlage führte zu dem Wunsch, diese Idee zu kodifizieren und ihr zu internationalem Recht zu verhelfen.

Die Welterbekonvention verpflichtet nicht nur ihre Mitgliedsstaaten zu aktiven und solidarischen Schutzmaßnahmen, sie bindet auch internationale nicht-staatliche Organi-

ideas were not implemented within international law. Only in our century were international legal instruments introduced for the protection of cultural properties, once the public had become alarmed at the heavy loss of the most beautiful and important cultural and natural properties in our supposedly civilized world.

The perilous existence of essential and irreplaceable things such as the diversity of species, and the threat to the creative development necessary for cultural diversity, eventually led to new concepts and the first – albeit tentative – international activities.

Hence the acceptance of the World Heritage Convention by UNESCO (1972) was the logical result of the successful and, up to that point, unique international campaign to save the temples of Abu Simbel in Upper Egypt. The temples had been placed under threat by flood from rising waters following the erection of the Aswan High Dam, and could only be safeguarded through costly intervention.

Here, for the first time, was proof that the international community was willing to acknowledge a joint heritage, and to raise the funds necessary for its protection. The successful saving of the temples led to the desire to establish a code enshrining the idea and to give this code an international legal dimension.

The World Heritage Convention not only obliges its member states to implement active protection measures with solidarity, but also encompasses non-governmental organizations such as the International Union for Conservation of Nature and Natural Resources (IUCN), the International Council for Museums (ICOMOS) and the International Centre for the Study of the Preservation and the Restoration of Cultural Property in Rome (ICCROM) in their work. All these organiza-

sationen, wie z. B. die Internationale Union zum Schutz der Natur (IUCN), den Internationalen Rat für Denkmalpflege (ICOMOS) und das sogenannte Rom-Zentrum zur Ausbildung von Fachkräften (ICCROM), in ihre Arbeit ein. Diese Organisationen, parlamentarische, lokale und regionale Verbände, die Medien, Jugendvereinigungen – sie alle spielen eine tragende Rolle beim Schutz der natürlichen Schönheit der Welt und ihrer geschichtlichen Zeugnisse. Die Bemühungen dieser verschiedenen Institutionen bleiben jedoch nutzlos, wenn diese nicht von der breiten Bevölkerung mitgetragen werden.

Die Welterbekonvention basiert auf der Idee, dass gewisse Natur- und Kulturstätten von „außergewöhnlichem, universellem Wert" sind und Teil des gemeinsamen Nachlasses der Menschheit darstellen. Die Erhaltung dieses gemeinsamen Erbes ist nicht nur Aufgabe der einzelnen Nationen, sondern aller Individuen. Einmalig ist auch die Tatsache, dass sowohl Kultur- als auch Naturgüter geschützt werden sollen. Angesichts der Wechselbeziehung zwischen Mensch und Natur ist dieser ganzheitliche Ansatz logisch und revolutionär zugleich. Beachtenswert ist an der Konvention auch, dass sie eine systematische Zusammenarbeit der Staatengemeinschaft im Bereich der Erhaltung von Kulturgütern ermöglicht hat. Jährlich bewilligt das 21-köpfige zwischenstaatliche Welterbekomitee einen Fonds zur Rettung von bedrohten Welterbestätten und zur Unterstützung gemeinsamer weltweiter Aktivitäten zum Schutz des Welterbes. Finanzielle Unterstützung erfahren auch Kurse für die Erhaltung von Kulturgütern, Vorbereitungsarbeiten für die Aufnahme von Kultur- und Naturgütern in die Welterbeliste und die ständige Beobachtung des Erhaltungszustandes derjenigen Güter, die bereits auf der

tions, parliamentary, local and regional associations, the media, and youth organizations play a vital role in the preservation of the natural beauty of the world and its historical evidence. However, even the best efforts of these institutions cannot succeed unless they are supported by the wider public as well.

The World Heritage Convention is based on the idea that certain natural and cultural sites are of "exceptional universal value" and part of a joint heritage of mankind. The preservation of this joint heritage is not just the task of the individual nations but of all individuals. The notion that both cultural and natural property should be protected is also unique. In the face of the correlation between man and nature, this comprehensive approach seems both revolutionary and logical. It is also remarkable that this convention gave rise to a systematic collaboration in the community within the field of preservation of cultural properties. Each year the International World Heritage Committee, consisting of 21 people, grants the funds to save threatened world heritage sites and to support worldwide joint activities for the protection of world heritage. Also awarded financial support are special training courses for the preservation of cultural and natural property, preparation work for the inscription of cultural and natural property on the World Heritage List and the continuous observation of those properties already on the list, and which must remain protected.

To date, 630 sites of exceptional universal value have been listed. They are located in 118 countries; 480 of them are cultural, 128 natural and 22 sites belong to both categories.

Despite moves towards a more balanced geographical representation of the listed

Liste stehen und unbedingt geschützt werden sollen.

Bis heute wurden 630 Stätten von außergewöhnlichem, universellem Wert in die Liste eingetragen. Diese befinden sich in 118 Ländern; 480 von ihnen sind Kulturgüter, 128 Naturgüter, und 22 Stätten gehören beiden Kategorien an.

Trotz Anstrengungen zu einer besseren geographischen Ausgewogenheit der aufgenommenen Welterbestätten, liegt der Schwerpunkt immer noch auf Westeuropa. In Zukunft sollten bei der Auswahl mehr Stätten aus den arabischen Ländern, aus dem Pazifikraum und aus Afrika berücksichtigt werden. Ein Teil dieses Erbes ist heute bedroht, und es bedarf beträchtlicher Anstrengungen zur längerfristigen Rettung solcher Stätten. Und Bedrohungen gibt es täglich neue. Das Welterbekomitee hat 27 Stätten, die akut bedroht sind, in die Liste des gefährdeten Welterbes, die sogenannte „Rote Liste", aufgenommen. Besonderen Anlass zur Besorgnis gibt der desolate Zustand der Weltnaturerbestätten im sog. demokratischen, von Kriegswirren heimgesuchten Kongo sowie der Schutz und Erhaltungszustand so bedeutender Kulturerbestätten wie Angkor/Kambodscha, Timbuktu/Mali, Butrint/Albanien und Hampi/Indien. Zwischenstaatliche Kriege und innerstaatliche Konflikte, die Zunahme des Massentourismus sowie unkontrollierte Entwicklungsprojekte erschweren zudem den Schutz der Kultur- und Naturgüter, die unser aller Welterbe darstellen.

Mit ihrer Anerkennung als Weltkulturerbe kann sich die Altstadt von Graz mit den bedeutendsten Kultur- und Naturgütern der Erde messen. Sie steht in einer Reihe mit den historischen Bauten von Venedig, Florenz, Krakau, Kyoto und Paris, aber auch mit so beeindruckenden Bauwerken wie der chine-

world heritage sites, the focus still rests mainly on Europe. In future, however, more sites in the Arabian countries, the Pacific and Africa are to be considered for selection. Part of this heritage is threatened today and major efforts are needed for the long-term preservation of sites of this kind. Each and every day new threats emerge. The World Heritage Committee has put 27 acutely-threatened sites on the list of world heritage at risk, the so-called "Red List". The dismal state of the world natural heritage sites subject to heavy civil wars in the so-called Democratic Congo is of particular concern. As is the state of preservation and upkeep of important cultural heritage sites such as Angkor/Cambodia, Timbuktu/Mali, Butrint/Albania and Hampi/India. Wars with other countries and internal conflict, the increase in mass tourism and uncontrolled development projects further adversely affect the preservation of the cultural and natural properties that are our world heritage.

With the recognition of its status as world cultural heritage, the old city of Graz has been classed alongside the most famous natural and cultural properties in the world. Not only has it been placed on a par with the historical buildings of Venice, Florence, Krakow, Kyoto and Paris, but also with such formidable constructions as the Chinese Wall, the Egyptian Pyramids and the Taj Mahal. The world heritage sites of Bamberg, Bern and Salzburg are most closely related to Graz in terms of their historical architectural urban development.

The wide diversity of world heritage properties is also highlighted by the fact that, at the same time as Graz, remarkably different sites were inscribed on the list in Marrakech (in December 1999). These are, for example, the Darjeeling Himalayas Railway in India,

sischen Mauer, den ägyptischen Pyramiden und dem Taj Mahal. Graz am stärksten verwandt in der historisch-architektonischen Stadtentwicklung sind die Welterbestätten Bamberg, Bern und Salzburg.

Das breite Spektrum der Welterbegüter wird auch deutlich, wenn wir uns vor Augen führen, dass gleichzeitig mit der Altstadt von Graz auch ganz anders geartete Stätten in Marrakesch (Dezember 1999) in die Welterbeliste aufgenommen wurden wie z. B.: die Darjeeling-Himalaya-Eisenbahn in Indien, übrigens die zweite Bahn auf der Welterbeliste nach der Semmeringbahn, die bereits 1998 als Welterbe anerkannt wurde; die Weinberge von Saint-Émilion in Frankreich, damit zum ersten Mal die Aufnahme einer vom Weinbau geprägten Kulturlandschaft; die Altstadt von Diamantina in Brasilien, Hortobágy National Park in Ungarn und die durch Luther bekannte mittelalterliche Feste Wartburg, im Osten Deutschlands gelegen.

Die Bedeutung der Welterbeliste kann daran gemessen werden, dass sie jenes Erbe der Menschheit erhält, das über alle politischen und kulturellen Gegensätze hinweg von der internationalen Staatengemeinschaft als schützenswert erklärt wurde. Die internationale Zusammenarbeit bei der Umsetzung der Welterbekonvention ist deshalb auch von der Achtung und Bewahrung der kulturellen Zeugnisse der anderen Kulturen geprägt. Sie wird durch einen intensiven, weltumspannenden kulturellen Dialog, der die Identität des Anderen anerkennt, möglich. Die Konvention ist ein Aufruf zur Toleranz und ein Beitrag zum Frieden.

Heute ist die Welterbekonvention mit ihren 158 Mitgliedsstaaten das erfolgreichste internationale Instrument zum Schutz von Kultur- und Naturgütern. Östrreich ist seit 1993 Mitglied der Konvention. Fünf österreichische

which incidentally, after the Semmering Railway (listed in 1998), is the second railway to be included in the list; the vineyards of Saint Emilion in France – the first listing of a landscape characterized by viniculture; the historic city of Diamantina in Brazil; the Hortobágy National Park in Hungary; and the mediaeval fortification of Wartburg in Eastern Germany, made famous by Martin Luther.

A measure of the importance of the World Heritage List is the fact that it preserves the heritage of mankind declared, beyond all political and cultural differences, worthy of protection by the community of states. Hence international collaboration in the implementation of the World Heritage Convention is also characterized by a respect for, and preservation of, the cultural evidence of other cultures. This stems from an intensive, worldwide cultural dialogue which recognizes the identity of "the other". The convention is an appeal for tolerance, and a contribution to peace.

Today, with 158 member states, the World Heritage Convention is the single most effective vehicle for the protection of cultural and natural properties. Austria has been a member of the convention since 1993 and to date five Austrian sites have been listed, including the Schloss and park of Schönbrunn, the historic city of Salzburg, the cultural landscape Hallstadt-Dachstein and last year the Semmering railway. It is widely recognized that world heritage sites are particularly vulnerable to innumerable dangers and threats in times of war and political conflict. The Red List previously mentioned includes critically endangered sites. So, although it is a great pleasure that Graz should be acknowledged as world cultural heritage, we must not forget that UNESCO focuses primarily on the prevention of war; it supports, and where neces-

Stätten wurden bislang auf die Welterbeliste gesetzt; darunter Schloss und Park von Schönbrunn, die Altstadt von Salzburg, die Kulturlandschaft Hallstadt-Dachstein und letztes Jahr die Semmeringbahn. Es ist gemeinhin bekannt, dass Welterbestätten vor allem in Kriegs- und Konfliktszeiten zahllosen Gefahren und Bedrohungen ausgesetzt sind: Die rote Liste des gefährdeten Welterbes ist weiter oben schon erwähnt. Bei aller Freude über die Anerkennung der historischen Altstadt von Graz als Welterbestätte sollten wir deshalb nicht vergessen, dass es das zentrale Anliegen der UNESCO bleibt, Kriege zu verhindern, und die Anerkennung der Rechte von Minderheiten und ihrer Kulturen zu unterstützen und – wo nötig – zu erkämpfen. Die Aufnahme in die Welterbeliste verpflichtet die Verantwortlichen zum vollständigen und dauerhaften Schutz dieses Welterbes. Es gilt zum Beispiel bei der Planung für die Altstadt Graz auch in der Zukunft stets feinfühlig vorzugehen, den richtigen Maßstab zu wahren und den Bürger zu beteiligen.

Bernd von Droste zu Hülshoff
Ehemals Beigeordneter Generaldirektor der UNESCO und Gründungsdirektor des UNESCO Zentrums für den Erhalt des Kultur- und Naturerbes der Menschheit.

sary even fights for, the recognition of minorities and their cultures. The inscription of Graz on the World Heritage List obliges those responsible to ensure the complete and continuous protection of world heritage. This means for example that for the future development of the historic city of Graz, plans must be sensitive to the surroundings, and in the right measure, and with the consideration of its inhabitants.

Bernd von Droste zu Hülshoff
Former Vice-General Director of the UNESCO and Foundation Director of the UNESCO Center for the Preservation of the Cultural and Natural Heritage of Mankind

City Profile of Graz

Stadtportrait Graz | III

City profile of Graz

Stadtportrait Graz

Blick in die Herrengasse
View of Herrengasse

Die Altstadt von Graz ist Mittelpunkt der gleichnamigen Landeshauptstadt des Bundeslandes Steiermark in der Republik Österreich.

Graz liegt auf den folgenden geographischen Koordinaten:

> Südlichster Punkt:
> geographische Länge: 15° 27' 42"
> geographische Breite: 47° 00' 44"
> Westlichster Punkt:
> geographische Länge: 15° 21' 03"
> geographische Breite: 47° 06' 25"
> Nördlichster Punkt:
> geographische Länge: 15° 24' 07"
> geographische Breite: 47° 08' 06"
> Östlichster Punkt:
> geographische Länge: 15° 32' 07"
> geographische Breite: 47° 06' 00"

The historic center of Graz is the core of the eponymous Styrian capital, Styria being one of the provinces (Länder) of the Republic of Austria.

In geographical terms, Graz is located within the following co-ordinates:

> Southernmost point:
> degree of longitude: 15° 27' 42"
> degree of latitude: 47° 00' 44"
> Westernmost point:
> degree of longitude: 15° 21' 03"
> degree of latitude: 47° 06' 25"
> Northernmost point:
> degree of longitude: 15° 24' 07"
> degree of latitude: 47° 08' 06"
> Easternmost point:
> degree of longitude: 15° 32' 07"
> degree of latitude: 47° 06' 00"

Luftbild Stadt Graz | The city of Graz, aerial view

III

Blick zum Schlossberg mit Franziskanerkirche
View of Schlossberg and Franciscan Church

Mit etwa einer Viertel Million Einwohnern ist Graz die zweitgrößte Stadt Österreichs und liegt im spannungsreichen Großraum zwischen Donauraum und Adria, am Schnittpunkt zwischen West- und Südosteuropa.

Die Stadt an der Grenze ist zugleich Stätte des Vermittelns, eine Funktion, die Graz seit dem Mittelalter als bedeutendste multikulturelle Drehscheibe im Alpen-Adria-Raum ausweist. Als Universitäts- und Kulturstadt ist Graz Knotenpunkt innerhalb eines kulturellen Städtenetzes, das sich von München bis Temesvar und Pécs, von Lemberg bis Pula und Triest, von Brünn bis Sarajewo und Dubrovnik, von Krakau bis Laibach und Zagreb erstreckt.

So erfüllte die Stadt seiner geographischen Lage entsprechend traditionsgemäß seit dem 14. Jahrhundert eine kulturelle und geistige Vormachtstellung.

Als Residenzstadt von Innerösterreich gewann sie fast über den gesamten Alpen-Adria-Raum überragende geistige Strahlkraft, stets offen für fremdes und neues Gedankengut, die eigene Identität durch Vielfalt bereichernd. Eine mentale Grundhaltung, ein geistiges grazerisches Phänomen, das, unvergleichlich im europäischen Städtereigen, in der Baukultur am elementarsten zum Ausdruck kommt.

An einem Knotenpunkt von Verkehrswegen gelegen, die schon seit der Vorgeschichte begangen wurden, an der vom Schlossberg geschüzten Murfurt, siedelten schon seit der Bronzezeit Menschen. Städtischen Charakter gewannen diese Siedlungen erst im Mittelalter. Aber nicht das Mittelalter, sondern das 16. Jahrhundert, die Renaissance, sollte für die Persönlichkeit der Stadt ausschlaggebend werden.

Das 16. und 17. Jahrhundert waren die Blütezeit der Stadt – bestimmt durch ihre

With about a quarter of a million inhabitants, Graz is Austria's second largest city and lies in between the captivating areas of the Danubian and Adriatic nations, at the intersection of west and south-east Europe.

This city on the border is also a place of encounter, a function that has made Graz a major multi-cultural pivot within the Alpine Adriatic region since medieval times. A university city, a city of the arts, Graz is junction in a cultural city network reaching from Munich to Temesvar and Pecs, from Lvov to Pula and Trieste, from Brno to Sarajevo and Dubrovnik, from Krakow to Ljubljana and Zagreb.

Due to its geographical position, the city has had a strong tradition of cultural and spiritual leadership since the 14th century.

At that time Graz was the residence of Inner Austria. As such it gained spiritual pre-eminence within the entire Alpine Adriatic region, developing an open-mindedness towards unknown and novel ideas and the ability to absorb them in order to enrich its own identity. This mental disposition, specifically a Graz phenomenon unparalleled by any other European city, is expressed in the most elementary way in the city's architectural heritage.

Situated at a junction of transit routes used since early history, the Schlossberg-protected Mur ford was first settled in the Bronze Age. It took until the Middle Ages for these settlements to evolve into a town proper.

However, it was not the Middle Ages but the 16th-century Renaissance that defined the city.

Its heyday came in the 16th and 17th centuries when Graz was once again a residence, when the fortifications against the Turks – who never actually besieged the city – were significantly enlarged, when the whole city

Schutzzonenplan | Protection Zone Map

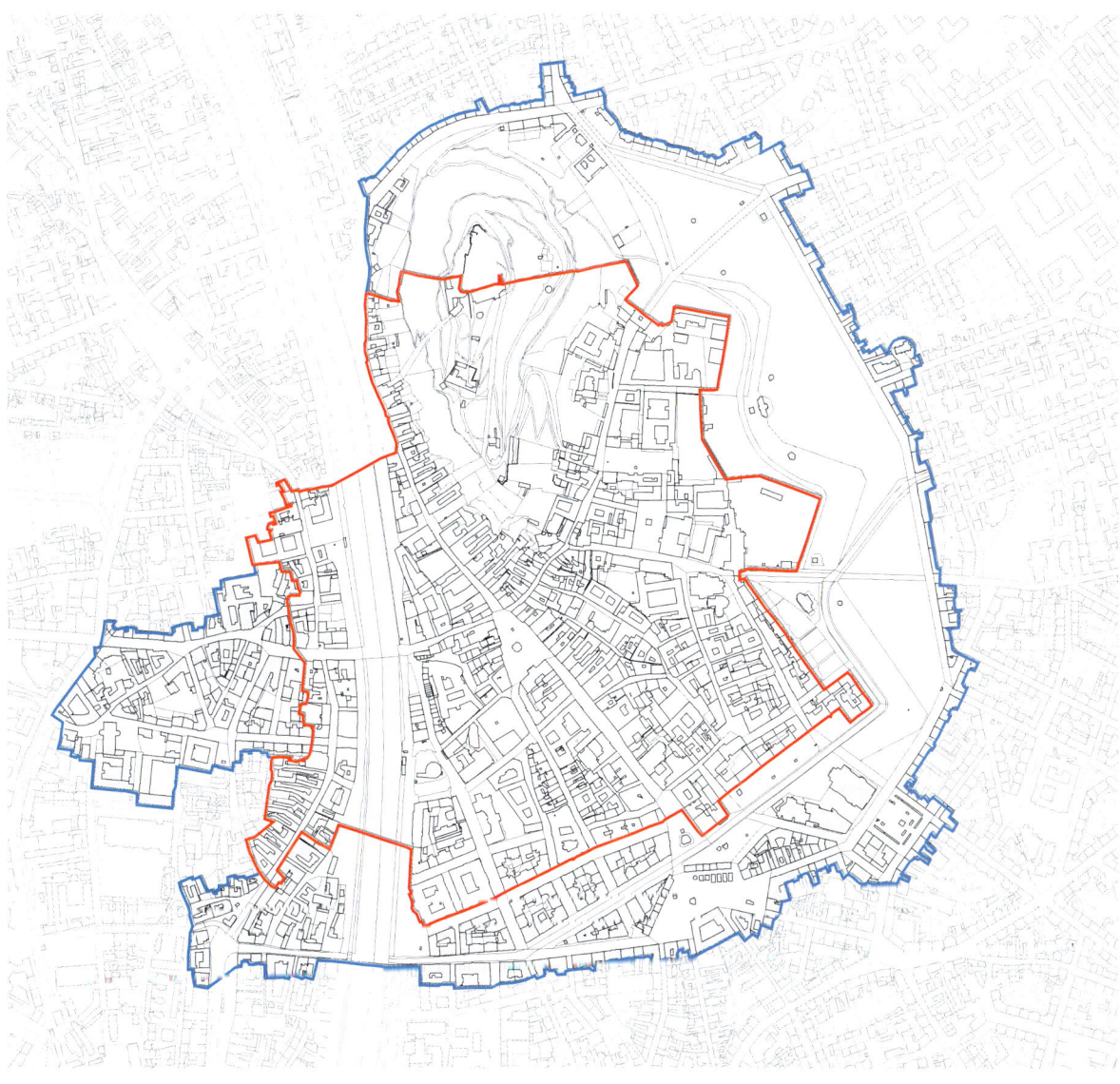

▬ Schutzzone 1: Historische Altstadt und rechtes Murufer
Protection zone I: Historic old town and right bank of the river Mur

▬ Pufferzone 2: II. und III. Bezirk, Gründerzeitviertel des 19. Jahrhunderts
Bufferzone 2: II. and III. area, boom-time 19th-century development

Quelle: Magistrat Graz, Stadtvermessungsamt/Stadtplanungsamt | Source: Graz City Council, City surveying and planning office

Rolle als Residenzstadt, durch den großzügigen Ausbau der Festungsanlage gegen die Türken, die die Stadt allerdings nie belagerten, die weitgehende Stadterneuerung, getragen von italienischen Bauleuten, definiert durch ihre Funktion als früher Kristallisationspunkt der weltpolitischen Auseinandersetzung zwischen Protestanten und Katholiken. Diese große Zeit ist bis heute in der Bausubstanz der inneren Stadt präsent.

Mit der Vertreibung der Protestanten, mit dem Abwandern des Hofes nach Wien beginnt eine ruhigere Phase der barocken Umformung, des weiteren Ausbaues der Stadt in kleinerem Umfang, immer noch getragen von den italienischen Künstlern und Handwerkern.

Dieses Zurücksinken der politischen Bedeutung von Graz erwies sich als konservierender Faktor. Erst als die gewaltigen Festungsmauern als Bedingung eines Friedensvertrages fielen, veränderte sich der Charakter der Stadt durch die Begrünung der frei werdenden Flächen. Dadurch fanden die Verbauungen des 19. und frühen 20. Jahrhunderts vorwiegend außerhalb des ehemaligen Glacis statt.

So kann Graz ein weitgehend ungestörtes urbanes Ensemble vorweisen, das in seiner Geschlossenheit seinesgleichen sucht. Dieses Ensemble ist ein Dokument der natürlichen Gegebenheiten des Geländes, der Fernwirkungen der europäischen Geschichte und des Gestaltungswillens der Grazer Bürger.

Die Schutzzonen:
Die Fläche der durch die Republik Österreich zur Aufnahme in die World Heritage List vorgesehenen Altstadt von Graz beträgt in der Schutzzone 719.700,60 m^2; diejenige der Pufferzone umfaßt insgesamt 757.233,34 m^2 (siehe Plan Seite 19).

Für die Festlegung der Schutzzone (Plan

was renewed, according in most instances to Italian builders' designs. This was also the time when Graz was defined by its role as the place where the global political conflict between Protestants and Catholics crystallized. This great era is still reflected in today's historic building fabric in the town centre.

Following the expulsion of the Protestants and the move of the imperial court to Vienna, the city entered a quieter period of Baroque alterations and modest growth, still however influenced heavily by the Italian artists and craftsmen.

This decline in political status had a strong conservational impact on Graz. It was only when the enormous fortification walls had to be razed in order to fulfil the condition of a peace treaty that the character of the city changed: the vacated areas were turned into a green belt, while 19th- and early 20th-century construction was focused outside the former glacis. This is why Graz boasts a largely unspoilt old-town ensemble unparalleled in its integrity. This assembly bears witness to the natural properties of the terrain, the remote effects of European history and the creative will of the Graz people.

The area of the historic center of Graz proposed for inclusion on the World Heritage List covers 719,700.60 m^2; the area of the buffer zone covers a total of 757,233.34 m^2 (map page 19).

In order to define the boundaries of the zone (map page 19, red line) of the historic center area, we have used as a reference the sites of the former fortifications built after 1546 by mainly Italian master builders. They are still partially in place at the eastern end of the historic center and can be easily identified in the line of buildings along Burgring – Opernring – Kaiserfeldgasse. Also, parts of the left Mur banks, the "Murvorstadt", or Mur vil-

Stadtentwicklung | City Development

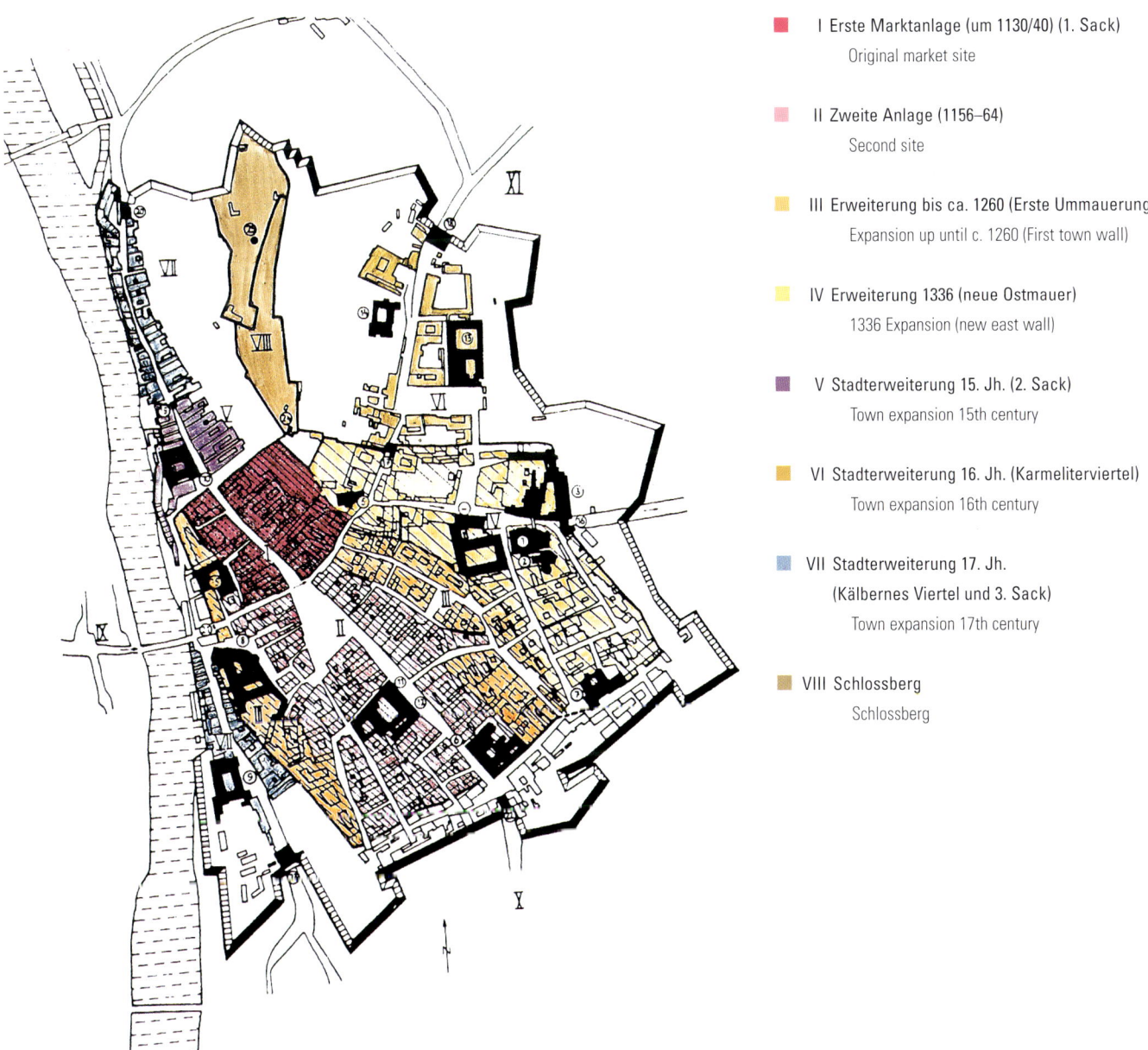

- I Erste Marktanlage (um 1130/40) (1. Sack)
  Original market site

- II Zweite Anlage (1156–64)
  Second site

- III Erweiterung bis ca. 1260 (Erste Ummauerung)
  Expansion up until c. 1260 (First town wall)

- IV Erweiterung 1336 (neue Ostmauer)
  1336 Expansion (new east wall)

- V Stadterweiterung 15. Jh. (2. Sack)
  Town expansion 15th century

- VI Stadterweiterung 16. Jh. (Karmelitierviertel)
  Town expansion 16th century

- VII Stadterweiterung 17. Jh.
  (Kälbernes Viertel und 3. Sack)
  Town expansion 17th century

- VIII Schlossberg
  Schlossberg

Quelle: Baualterplan nach F. Posch, Stadtmuseum Graz | Source: Building age plan after F. Posch, Graz City Museum

III

Opernringverbauung
Opernring assembly

Barmherzigenkirche
Barmherzigenkirche

Seite 19, rote Linie) des engeren historischen Altstadtgebietes war zunächst der Verlauf der ab 1546 vorwiegend von italienischen Baumeistern errichteten Befestigungsanlagen maßgebend, die am östlichen Ende der Altstadt noch zum Teil vorhanden und auch an der Verbauungslinie Burgring–Opernring–Kaiserfeldgasse deutlich ablesbar sind. Ebenso wurden jene Teile des rechten Murufers, die sog. Murvorstadt, in den Altstadtbezirk einbezogen, die an der historischen, vom Lendplatz zum Griesplatz verlaufenden Nord-Süd-Straße gelegen sind. Dieser Straßenzug (Mariahilfer Straße–Griesgasse) folgt der einstigen Topographie des Mur-Ufer-Verlaufes und wird fast durchwegs beiderseits von historischen Bauten begrenzt. Durch dieses Übergreifen der Zone in den „Brückenkopf" des rechten Murufers – hier war der mit der Entstehung der Stadt ursächlich verbundene Flussübergang situiert – wird der einheitlichen Verbauung an beiden Seiten des Flusses Rechnung getragen.

Die im Plan ausgewiesene Pufferzone (blaue Linie) umfasst einerseits die bewaldete Nordflanke des Schlossberges, den Stadtpark und im Wesentlichen jene Verbauung, die nach der Aufhebung der Stadtbefestigungen in der ersten Hälfte des 19. Jahrhunderts entstanden ist. Sie ist gekennzeichnet durch Bauwerke des späten Klassizismus und des frühen Historismus, die den Altstadtkern in einem geschlossenen Ring umgeben. Am rechten Murufer ist in die Schutzzone die historische Verbauung des Andrä-Viertels, die Bürgerspitalsstiftung, der Bereich um die Barmherzigenkirche und die Mariahilferkirche mit dem Minoritenkloster einbezogen.

lage, have been included in the nominated area. They are located along the streets running from Lendplatz to Griesplatz in a north-south direction. This line of streets (Mariahilfer Strasse–Griesgasse) follows the former topography of the Mur banks and is bordered on both sides by an almost uninterrupted array of historic buildings. By projecting the zone into the "bridgehead" of the right Mur bank – this is the site of the original ford from which the city spread – we pay due regard to the uniform cityscape on both sides of the river.

The buffer zone (blue line) shown in the map encompasses the wooded northern flank of the Schlossberg, the City Park, plus a major portion of the buildings constructed in the first half of the 19th century following the demolition of the city fortifications. These are buildings of late Classicism and early Historicism encircling the historic center core. On the right bank of the Mur the buffer zone includes the historic buildings of the Andrä quarter, the Burghers' Hospice Foundation and the ecclesiastical precinct of the hospitallers' church and monastery (Barmherzigenkirche and Barmherzigenkloster).

Denkmalschutzplan | Monument Protection Plan

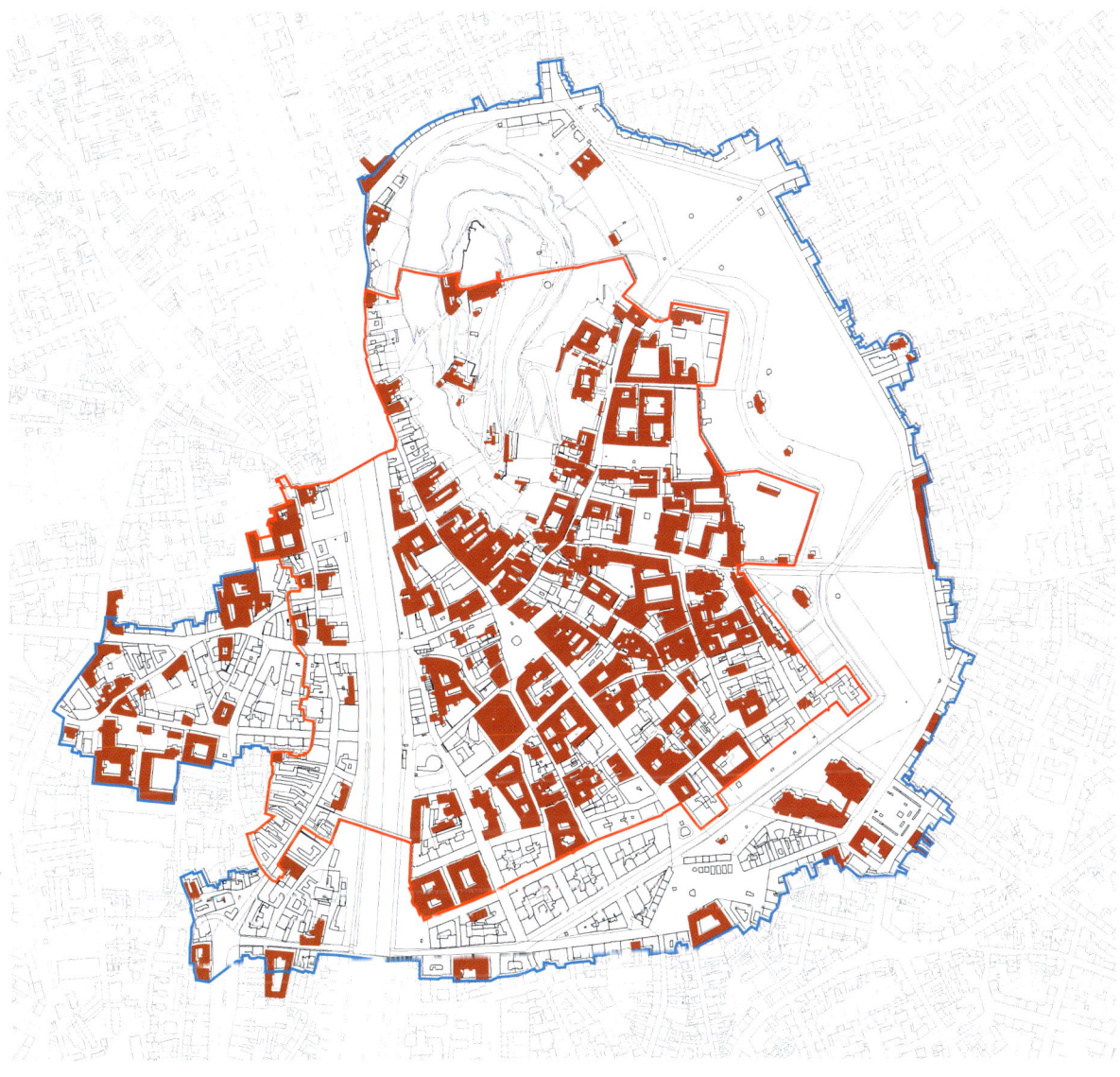

■ Denkmalschutz | Monument protection

Quelle: Magistrat Graz, Stadtvermessungsamt/Stadtplanungsamt | Source: Graz City Council, City surveying and planning office

Übersichtsplan | Overall Plan

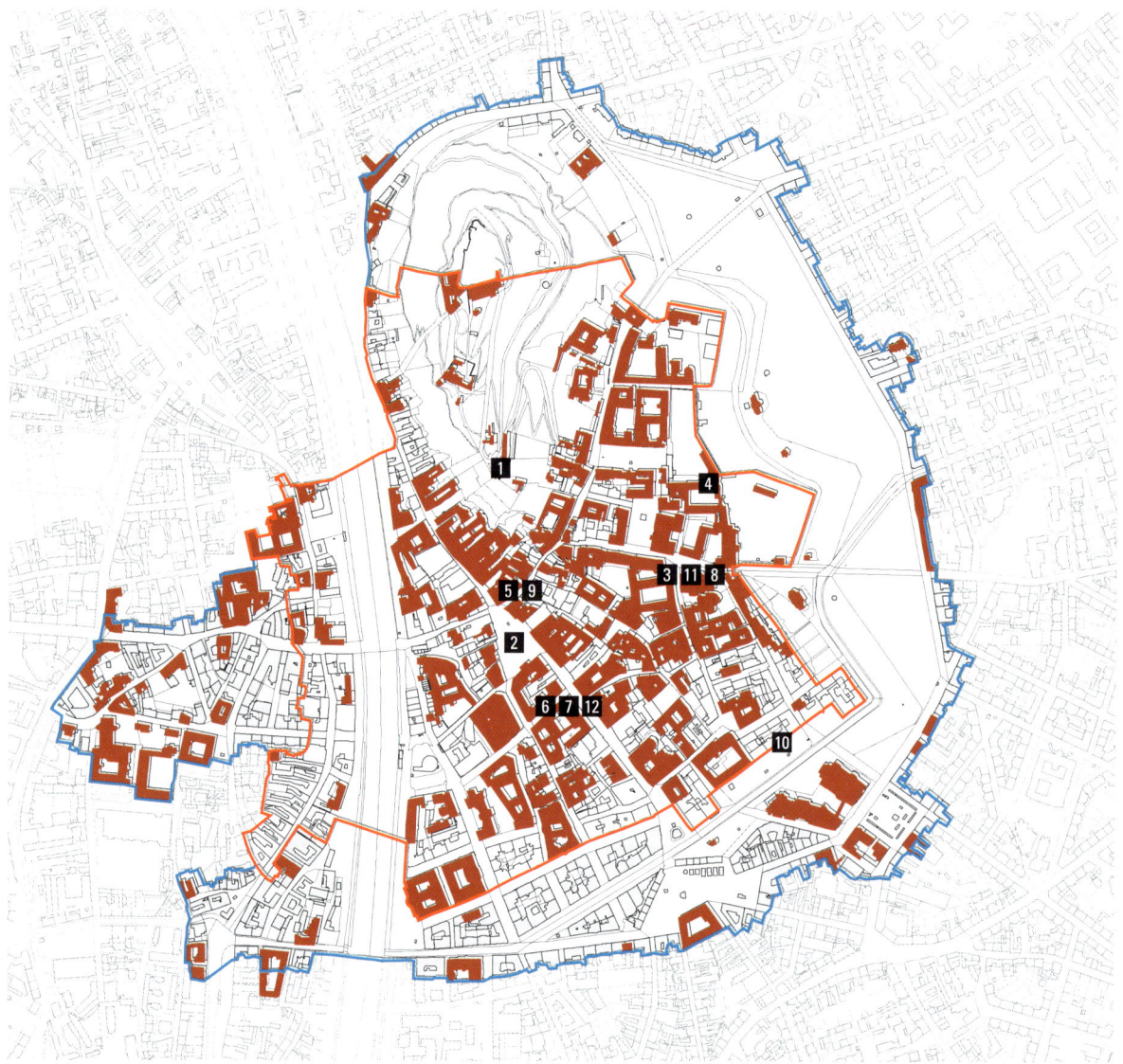

Quelle: Magistrat Graz, Stadtvermessungsamt/Stadtplanungsamt | Source: Graz City Council, City surveying and planning office

Legende | Legend

1 Grazer Uhrturm auf dem Schlossberg, um 1570
   Graz Clock Tower on the Schlossberg (castle hill), about 1570

2 Hauptplatz mit Rathaus, mittelalterliche Hofstättenanlagen in Sporgasse, Sackstraße
   Hauptplatz (main square) with Rathaus (city hall), medieval courtyards in Sporgasse, Sackstraße

3 Stadtkrone mit Dom, Mausoleum, Priesterseminar, Burg
   The Town Crown with the cathedral, mausoleum, seminary, Burg (castle)

4 Doppelwendeltreppe, Grazer Burg, 1499
   Double-spiral staircase, Graz Burg, 1499

5 Ehem. Deutschordenshaus 15./16. Jh.
   Courtyard of the house of the Teutonic Order of Knights

6 Landhaus, Landeszeughaus (16.–17. Jh.)
   Landhaus (seat of regional government), Armoury, 16th-17th century

7 Landeszeughaus, Waffenkammer, (17. Jh.), Herrengasse
   Landeszeughaus, armoury, (17th century), Herrengasse

8 Mausoleum, Fassade mit Katharinenkirche (17. Jh.)
   Mausoleum, façade with the Church of St. Catherine, (17th century)

9 Jugendstilfassade um 1900, Sporgasse
   Art nouveau façade about 1900, Sporgasse

10 Opernringverbauung, (19. Jh.)
   Opernring construction (19th century)

11 Grazer Dom, gotisches Hauptportal
   Cathedral, Gothic main portal

12 Landhaushof, Renaissancearkadenhof
   Landhaus courtyard, Renaissance arcades

Begründung für die Aufnahme der Altstadt von Graz in die World Heritage List

Graz von Süden um 1626/1657,
Laurenz van de Sype/Wenzel Hollar,
Kupferstich

View of Graz from the south, c. 1626–57,
Laurenz van de Sype/Wenzel Hollar, engraving

„Mit ihren historischen Baudenkmälern, ihrem italienisch anmutenden Charakter, dem Wechselspiel zwischen engen Gassenschluchten und lichten, weiten Plätzen, mit ihrem Charme und ihrer Anziehungskraft auf Gäste und Besucher zählt die Altstadt von Graz zu den bedeutendsten Stadtensembles von Österreich.

Der Altstadtbereich hat sich – trotz mancher Zeugnisse von Nachkriegs- und zeitgenössischer Architektur ringsum – wohltuend abgeschirmt, einerseits durch den Schlossberg, andererseits durch die rasterförmig angelegte Vorstadt des 19. Jahrhunderts, die einheitlich und ungestört bewahrt werden konnte.

Um zwei urbane Zellen fügten die Jahrhunderte Stadtstruktur und -architektur. Die eine bildet der Markt mit dem Hauptplatz als mittelalterliche planmäßige Anlage, also die Altstadt, geschützt vom Schlossberg. Die an-

"With its historic monuments, Italian atmosphere, the interplay between narrow streets and bright wide squares, its specific charm and growing pull of attraction for visitors and guests, the historic center of Graz ranks among the most significant collection of town buildings of Austria.

The historic center area has, despite examples of post-war and contemporary architecture in its surroundings, remained happily sheltered by the Schlossberg and by the grid-patterned suburbs of the 19th century, allowing it to be preserved in its entirety and integrity.

Centuries of development have formed the city structure and architecture around two urban cells. One is the former market with the main square, a systematic medieval arrangement, i.e. the historic center at the foot of the Schlossberg. The other, majestically raised

Stadtbild mit Schlossberg und Murfluss, Luftbild, Blick nach Norden, 1990

View of Graz, Schlossberg and river Mur, aerial photograph, towards north, 1990

dere, leicht erhaben über der Stadt thronend, vereinigt geistige und weltliche Macht, also Dom und Burg, in einem einzigartigen Bauensemble, der sog. Stadtkrone.

Der Verlauf der ersten Gassenmarktanlage ist bis heute nachvollziehbar, sie zeichnet sich im Grundriss noch immer in der ältesten Verteilung der Hofstätten deutlich ab. Die mittelalterliche Stadtbefestigung, die sogenannte Ringmauer, ist nicht nur durch Pläne des 19. Jahrhunderts exakt rekonstruierbar, sondern teilweise auch noch in situ vorhanden, denn im Kern mittelalterliche Wehrtürme und Stadttore sind erhalten, ebenso wie Reste am östlichen Ende der Altstadt.

Mittelalterliche Bausubstanz ist im bürgerlichen Profanbereich überwiegend im Mauerwerk unverputzter Keller und im Erdgeschoßbereich fassbar, umfangreicher noch in der Burg und in den Stiftshöfen. Aus Spätgotik

above the town, unites spiritual and worldly power, church and ducal residence (Burg), into a unique complex called the crown of the town, or Stadtkrone.

How the ground plan of the first street market looked can still be seen in the earliest arrangement of homesteads. The medieval town fortifications, the so-called ring wall, can be fully reconstructed not only from 19th-century maps but also from its existing in-situ remnants: fortified medieval towers and town gates have been preserved, as have remnants at the eastern end of the historic center.

The original medieval material is mostly preserved in the masonry of unplastered cellars and in the ground floors of the secular burgher houses, even more so in the Burg and abbey courtyards. Graz boasts extraordinary examples of late Gothic and Renaissance ar-

III

Herrengasse, Landhaus, Landeszeughaus
Herrengasse, Landhaus, Armoury

und Renaissance sind in Graz hervorragende Baudenkmäler erhalten. Als bedeutendster Bau der Gegenreformation ist als ein Höhepunkt in der Stadtentwicklung das von den Jesuiten errichtete Grazer Kollegium zu nennen – der neben Augsburg, München und Koblenz größte Kollegiumsbau im deutschen Sprachraum. Von großer künstlerischer Bedeutung für das Stadtbild ist auch das Ensemble von Landhaus und Zeughaus mit dem prächtigen Arkadenhof, einer der wichtigsten Monumentalarchitekturen der Renaissance in Österreich.

Die Bauten, die in ihrem Renaissanceerscheinungsbild heute noch fassbar sind, in den Gewölbestrukturen der Erdgeschoßzonen und vor allem in den Innenhöfen mit Arkadengängen, erinnern an das besondere Charakteristikum einer norditalienischen Renaissancestadt. Besonders bemerkenswert

chitecture. A culmination in the town's development was the Jesuit College of Graz, the most significant building of the Counter-Reformation. After Augsburg, Munich and Koblenz, this is the largest college building in the German-speaking world. Of major artistic relevance for the urban streetscape is the ensemble formed by the Landhaus and Armoury with their magnificent arcaded yard, one of the most important examples of monumental Renaissance architecture north of the Alps.

The Renaissance buildings, whose original look is still apparent in the vault structures of the ground floor zones and especially in the arcaded inner courtyards, are evocative of the particular flair of a northern Italian Renaissance town. Of note are the Renaissance portals and sgraffito surfaces, some of them uncovered only recently in the course

III

Stadtkrone, Luftaufnahme mit Dom, Mausoleum und Priesterseminar

Stadtkrone, aerial photograph of the Cathedral, Mausoleum and Seminary

sind auch die Renaissanceportale und Sgraffiti, die – teilweise erst in den letzten Jahren – anlässlich von Restaurierungen zu Tage traten. Weitere Funde sind noch zu erwarten.
Weithin sichtbar sind zwei Monumentalbauten aus dem 17. Jahrhundert, die Jesuitenuniversität und das imperiale, in seiner Einzigartigkeit kunsthistorisch international bedeutende Mausoleum der Habsburger, dicht neben dem gotischen Dom situiert.
Vorhanden aus dem Barock sind noch eine Reihe von Adelspalästen mit stuckierten Fassaden und die besonders für Graz spezifischen großzügigen Treppenanlagen. Auch zahlreiche qualitätsvolle Bürgerhäuser des 18. Jahrhunderts beleben mit beachtenswerten Stuckdekorationen und repräsentativen Portalen das Stadtbild, im Inneren oft mit Wand- und Deckenausstattungen geschmückt.

of restorations. Further finds are expected.
Seen from a distance are two monumental buildings from the 17th century: the Jesuit university and the internationally unique and historically significant Mausoleum of the Habsburgs next to the Gothic cathedral.
Of Baroque origin are a number of townhouses of the aristocracy with their characteristic oriels and painted and stuccoed facades, so typical of the period, and the Graz-specific spacious staircases. Also numerous high-quality 18th-century burgher houses enliven the townscape with their remarkable stucco exteriors and impressive portals, in many instances also displaying fine wall and ceiling decorations inside.
Hence a variety of monuments from Baroque, Renaissance and medieval times form a unique urban ensemble with the Schlossberg as its unmistakable landmark and the Mur river

III

Dachlandschaft, Herrengasse mit Stadtpfarrkirche
Rooftops, Herrengasse and Parish Church

Dachlandschaft, Sackstraße
Rooftops, Sackstraße

Ein lebendiges Ineinander vielfältiger Baudenkmäler aus Barock, Renaissance und auch des Mittelalters fügt sich also in der Altstadt zu einem einzigartigen, vom Schlossberg dominierten und der Mur malerisch durchflossenen städtebaulichen Ensemble zusammen. Unter der vielgestaltigen eindrucksvollen Silhouette der Türme und Kuppeln der zahlreichen Kirchenbauten reihen sich die geschlossenen Fassadenprospekte der Adelspalais und Bürgerhäuser an Plätzen und verwinkelten engen Gassen in den historischen Stadtteilen, die auch über eine intakte Dachlandschaft verfügen.

Ein Blick auf Zone und Pufferzone läßt klar die nach Schleifung der Befestigung beibehaltene historische Trennung zwischen Altstadt und Vorstadt bzw. gründerzeitliche Stadterweiterung erkennen. Die Pufferzone ergibt sich, wie schon erwähnt, zum Teil durch die geographische Situation (Schlossberg), zum Teil durch die einheitliche Verbauung des 19. Jahrhunderts, die schon für sich durch ihre Ungestörtheit Einmaligkeit besitzt. In dieser rastermäßig angelegten Vorstadt befinden sich zudem so bemerkenswerte Bauwerke, wie etwa die mittelalterliche Leechkirche, einer der wichtigsten sakralen Bauten von Graz, oder die Oper.

Der hohe Anteil an Grünflächen (10.000 ha Gesamtgrünfläche sind 78 % der Grazer Stadtfläche, ein international unerreichter Wert) und deren hervorragende gärtnerische Gestaltung haben Graz die Bezeichnung einer „Gartenstadt" eingetragen. Der Schlossberg, eine Kulturlandschaft mit eigener Flora und Fauna seltener Pflanzen und Tiere, spielt als Krönung der grünen Oase des Stadtparks für die Erholung der Grazer eine wichtige Rolle. Umfangreiche Sanierungsarbeiten an allen wichtigen Gebäuden, Wegen und Steigen wurden mit großem finanziellen Aufwand

as its picturesque waterline. Among the varied and impressive silhouette of spires, towers and domes of numerous churches, we find the unspoiled facades of aristocratic townhouses and burgher houses which line pretty squares and crooked, narrow streets in the city's historic quarter and which feature an intact roofscape.

Taking a closer look at both the zone of the nominated property and the buffer zone, we recognise the historical borderline, as defined by the dismantled fortifications, between the historic center and the suburbs or boom-time (Gründerzeit) town development respectively. As already mentioned, the buffer zone results both from geographic position (Schlossberg) and from the uniform 19th-century city development, a unique example of an intact townscape in its own right. This grid-pattern suburb also includes a number of remarkable buildings, such as the medieval Leechkirche, one of the most important ecclesiastical buildings of Graz, and the opera house.

Graz is also called the "garden city". It owes this name to its numerous parks and green areas of outstanding design (totalling 10,000 ha or 78 % of the city's area, an internationally unparalleled ratio). A cultural landscape featuring its own flora and fauna of rare plants and animals, the Schlossberg is the highpoint of the green City Park oasis and a popular recreation area for the people of Graz. Much effort has been put into the extensive renovation projects on all important buildings, ways and paths in this area.

By way of summary one may say that the integrity and the variety of architectural styles and epochs displayed in Graz's historic center, which is of extraordinary cultural value, make it one of the most beautiful and outstanding properties in Europe. There are

Landhaus, Blick in den Arkadenhof
Landhaus, view of the arcaded courtyard

III

Der Hauptwachplatz (Hauptplatz),
um 1840, Conrad Kreuzer, Tempera

Hauptwachplatz (now the main square)
c. 1840, Conrad Kreuzer, distemper painting

Grazer Hauptplatz mit Schlossberg,
2000, Blick nach Nordosten

The main square and the Schlossberg
2000, view towards north-east

hier durchgeführt.

Zusammenfassend kann gesagt werden, dass die historisch außerordentlich wertvolle Altstadt von Graz in ihrer Geschlossenheit sowie in der Vielfalt der in ihr vertretenen architektonischen Stilepochen zu einer der schönsten und bedeutendsten in Europa zählt. Klar und lückenlos, wie vielleicht kaum anderswo, spiegelt sich im Stadtbild die Entwicklungsgeschichte wider. Eine jede Stilphase ist mit charakteristischen Gruppen von Baudenkmälern vertreten, die, einander ergänzend, sich zu einem einheitlich geschlossenen Ganzen zusammenfügen: Das ausgehende Mittelalter hinterließ mächtige Hallenkirchen, die Renaissance eine große Zahl stimmungsvoller Arkadenhöfe und das am stärksten vorherrschende Barock prächtige Adelspalais und Bürgerhäuser.

Gerade die Differenziertheit der Grazer Altstadt ist es auch, die im Rahmen wissenschaftlicher Untersuchungen stets betont wird. Das Nebeneinander unterschiedlicher stilistischer Elemente, das Aneinanderreihen von Bauten verschiedener Entstehungszeit und nicht zuletzt die ausgedehnten Gartenanlagen tragen zum Flair dieser Altstadt wesentlich bei."

Ernst Bacher, Generalkonservator,
Bundesdenkmalamt Wien

very few places where the town prospect mirrors the city's historical development so clearly and completely. Each style is represented by a characteristic group of monuments which complement each other and come together in a uniform and undisturbed whole: the late Middle Ages left its mighty hall churches, the Renaissance its numerous atmospheric arcaded yards and the predominant Baroque period its magnificent facades. It is this varied look of the historic center of Graz which is always emphasized in scientific papers and studies. The co-existence of a great variety of styles and their components, the integrity of rows of buildings from different epochs, and last but not least the extensive parks and gardens greatly contribute to the specific flair of the historic center."

Ernst Bacher, Head of Department for Conservation,
Federal Office of Historical Monuments

Description of the Historic Center of Graz

Beschreibung der Altstadt von Graz

IV

Beschreibung der Altstadt von Graz

Schlossberg mit Uhrturm, Franziskanerkirche

Schlossberg and Clock Tower, Franciscan Church

Geschichtliche Entwicklung

Frühzeit
Alpenslawen
Kolonisation

Die ältesten Spuren menschlicher Entwicklungen, die im heutigen Stadtgebiet gefunden wurden, entstammen der jüngeren Steinzeit. Diese und andere Depot- wie Gräberfunde weisen auf vorgeschichtliche Siedlungsbereiche am Westrand des Grazer Feldes an der vom Plabutsch überragten Hügelkette.
Hingegen kann Graz nicht, wie so manch andere österreichische Stadt, auf eine römische Siedlung als Vorgängerin hinweisen.
Als einzige Kontinuität aus der Antike ist hier ein lokaler Verkehrsweg erhalten geblieben, der im Mittelalter als „strata hungarica" bekannt, von Osten aus Pannonien kommend

Historical Development

Prehistoric times
Alpine Slavs
Colonisation

The earliest traces of human development found in today's municipal area date from the Neolithic period. These and other finds of graves and deposits of prehistoric artifacts indicate the existence of prehistoric settlements on the western border of the Grazer Feld at the foot of the chain of hills topped by the Plabutsch mountain.
Unlike several other Austrian cities, Graz does not date back to Roman settlement.
The only remnant of antiquity is a local trading route, known as the "strata hungarica" in the Middle Ages, which came from the east (Pannonia), entered the Grazer Feld near

IV

Kälbernes Viertel mit Franziskanerkirche
und Hauptplatz, Blick gegen Osten

„Kälbernes Viertel", Franciscan Church,
Hauptplatz, eastern view

bei St. Leonhard (römische Gräberfunde) das Grazer Feld betrat und an der heutigen Kreuzung Hofgasse-Sporgasse noch einen weiteren Verbindungsweg von Weiz aufnahm.
Weiter nach Westen verlaufend überschritt diese Verbindungsstraße zu Füßen des Schlossberges die Mur mit einer Furt, durchquerte das Grazer Feld, um im Westen auf die wichtige von Nord nach Süd ziehende Römerstraße zu stoßen.
Nach dem Untergang Roms folgte die Epoche der Völkerwanderung. Die von den Awaren abhängigen Alpen- oder Karantaner-Slawen kamen in die Steiermark und nach Kärnten und errichteten das Herzogtum Karantanien. Die Vernichtung des Awarenreiches durch Karl den Großen brachte zu Ende des 8. Jahrhunderts die Eingliederung Karantaniens unter fränkische Herrschaft.

St. Leonhard (Roman grave finds), then joined another road from Weiz at today's junction of Hofgasse and Sporgasse. Further to the west, at the foot of the Schlossberg, this road crossed the river Mur at a ford, then continued through the Grazer Feld, meeting in the west with the major Roman road running north to south.
The fall of Rome was followed by a period of the migration of peoples. The Alpine or Carantanian Slavs, dependent on the Avars, came to Styria and Carinthia and established the Duchy of Carantania. After Charlemagne had subjugated the Avars at the end of the 8th century, Carantania came under Frankish rule. However, the beginnings of German colonisation in the Eastern March were brought to an abrupt end by the Hungarian invasion in c. 900. It was only after the Hungarians had been defeated in 955 in the Battle

IV

Schlossberg, Grazer Uhrturm
Schlossberg, Clock Tower

Den Anfängen der deutschen Kolonisation in der Ostmark bereitete allerdings der Ungarneinbruch um 900 ein jähes Ende.

Erst als die Ungarn in der Schlacht auf dem Lechfeld 955 geschlagen wurden, konnte auch der Grazer Boden in das neuerrichtete Markensystem einbezogen werden. Nunmehr zur „Karantanischen Mark" gehörig, änderte sich die Situation des Grazer Raumes, dessen östliche Hügelkette bereits in den Grenzraum zum ungarischen Herrschaftsbereich überging.

Aus dieser Situation wird die Anlage eines kleinen Kastells auf dem Schlossberg deutlich, das in die zweite Hälfte des 10. Jahrhunderts zu datieren ist (heute nicht mehr vorhanden). Aus der Bezeichnung dieses Wehrbaues (gradec = kleine Burg) sollte sich auch der spätere Stadtname ableiten, eine der üblichen Erklärungen für die Namensfindung von Graz.

Der Grazer Boden gehörte zu diesem Zeitpunkt noch nicht den Landesfürsten, sondern einem einheimischen Geschlecht, den Hochfreien von Stübing, die ihre Herkunft von den Aribonen ableiteten. Diese errichteten auf dem Schlossberg zwischen 1125 und 1130 eine Herrschaftsburg. Parallel dazu ein Wirtschaftszentrum mit Meierhof und Kirche an der Stelle des heutigen Burg-Dom-Komplexes (siehe Stadtkrone). In diese Zeit fällt auch die erste urkundliche Erwähnung von Graz aus dem Jahre 1128/29.

Marktsiedlung und Stadtleben

Zu diesem Herrschaftszentrum entwickelte sich zwischen 1130 und 1140 ein erster Gassenmarkt (Bereich der heutigen Sackstraße, 1. Sack). Mit der Übernahme des Grazer Bodens durch den Traungauer Markgrafen

on the Lechfeld that the territory of Graz could be incorporated into the newly established system of marches. It was now part of the "Carantanian March". This changed the entire situation of the land surrounding Graz which on its eastern fringes already touched upon Hungarian territory.

This frontier situation explains the construction of a small fort on the Schlossberg in the second half of the 10th century, which has since vanished. One of the usual explanations given for the name of the town, Graz, is that it derived from this fort (gradec=small fortress).

At that time the land of Graz did not belong to the sovereign but to a local dynasty, the allodiaries of Stübing, who traced their descent from the Aribones. They built themselves a castle on the Schlossberg between 1125 and 1130, as well as domestic buildings including farm quarters and a church in the place of today's Burg–Cathedral complex (see "Stadtkrone"). It is at this time that Graz is first mentioned in a deed (1128/29).

Market Town and Town Life

The manorial complex soon gave rise to a street market which developed between 1130 and 1140 in the area of today's Sackstrasse (1st section or "Sack"). When Otakar III of Steyer (Styria), Margrave of the Traungau,

Gotische Leechkirche
Gothic Leechkirche

Ottokar III. von Steyr (Steiermark) war die Entwicklung von Graz als Landeshauptstadt der Steiermark gegeben.

Als Zeichen dafür ist die Anlage des großzügigen trapezförmigen Hauptplatzes (ursprünglich bis zur Landhausgasse reichend) zu sehen, der um 1164 im Anschluss an den alten Straßenmarkt entstand und an Größe alles Übrige im Lande übertraf.

Neben dem Adel stellten vor allem bürgerliche Gewerbetreibende und Händler das Gros der Bevölkerung. Eine wichtige Rolle vor allem als Geldgeber spielten die Juden, die bis zu ihrer Vertreibung am Ausgang des 15. Jahrhunderts in einem Ghetto wohnten.

Die ersten Vorstädte entstanden im Bereich von Mehlplatz und Färberplatz.

Außerhalb der ersten Stadtmauer von 1233 kam es zu Klostergründungen. Am sog. Leechhügel, einem seit der Bronzezeit be-

took possession of the land, this marked the beginning of the development of Graz into the capital of Styria. One sign of its new status was the large trapezoidal Hauptplatz (= main square – originally extending as far as Landhausgasse) built in c. 1164 next to the old street market. Its size was unsurpassed throughout the land.

Apart from the nobility, the major part of the population consisted of artisans and tradesmen. The Jews, who lived in a ghetto until their expulsion at the end of the 15th century, played an important role, primarily as money lenders.

The first villages outside the town walls appeared in the vicinity of Mehlplatz and Färberplatz. Monasteries formed outside the first town wall of 1233. The Teutonic Order founded the "Leech Commendam" on the so-called Leech Hill which had been used as a

IV

Reinerhof, urkundlich ältestes Gebäude der Stadt, Baukern 12. Jh., Umbauten 16.–19. Jh.

Reinerhof, oldest documented building, core structure dating from the 12th century, converted in the 16th to 19th centuries

nutzten Grabhügel (heutige Leechkirche) gründete der Deutsche Ritterorden die Commende Leech.

Auch die Klöster des Landes besaßen im ältesten Graz ihre wehrhaften Stadthöfe, die zur frühesten Bausubstanz von Graz gehören (siehe Reinerhof, ältestes urkundlich erwähntes Bauwerk in Graz).

Vom alten Zentrum lag die Pfarrkirche St. Ägydius (heutige Grazer Domkirche) noch außerhalb der Stadtmauern, diese wurde erst 1336 anlässlich einer umfangreichen Stadterweiterung nach Osten in die Stadtbefestigung mit einbezogen. Entsprechend seiner Verkehrssituation besaß Graz zunächst nur im Osten und Westen Tore (Paulustor, Burgtor, heute noch vorhanden, Murtor wurde abgebrochen).

Die Geschlechter der Traungauer und Babenberger herrschten auf Grazer Boden. Ab 1260 folgte der große Förderer des Städtewesens der Böhmenkönig Przemysl Ottokar II. als Stadtherr. Seit dieser Zeit besaß Graz die Stadtrechte und führte im Wappen den traungauischen Panther. Ab 1281 übernahm Rudolf I. von Habsburg die Belange der Stadt.

grave mound since the Bronze Age (today's Leechkirche). The monasteries also had well-fortified town residences inside Graz, which are among the oldest buildings still in existence (see Reinerhof, the oldest documented building in Graz).

Of the buildings which form part of the old centre, the parish church of St. Ägydius (today's Cathedral) lay outside the town walls. It was not incorporated into the municipal fortifications until 1336, when the town appropriated large tracts of land to the east. Reflecting its geographical position, Graz had town gates only at the eastern and western walls (Paulus Gate, Burg Gate, both still existing, while the Mur Gate was demolished).

The land of Graz was first ruled by the Traungau and Babenberg dynasties. They were followed in 1260 by the great patron of urban development, Przemysl Ottokar II, King of Bohemia. Graz received the status of town and was granted the use of the Traungau panther in its coat of arms. In 1281 Rudolf I of Habsburg succeeded him, also as ruler of the town.

Graz als Residenz

Bestimmend für die weitere urbane Entwicklung von Graz war vor allem der sog. Vertrag von Neuberg 1379, der eine Teilung des Habsburgerreiches vorsah. Die Stadt wurde zum Sitz der Leopoldinischen Linie der Habsburger.

Graz entwickelte sich damals zum kulturellen und geistigen Verwaltungszentrum „Innerösterreichs", das die Länder Steiermark, Kärnten, Krain, Istrien, Triest, Görz und Gradisca umfasste, diese waren im 16. und 17. Jahrhundert staatsrechtlich selbständig.

Graz – The Court Residence

The Treaty of Neuberg (1379), which provided for the partition of the Habsburg Empire, also determined the urban development of Graz. The town became the seat of the Habsburg line established by Leopold III, the administrative capital and cultural and intellectual centre of "Inner Austria", which included Styria, Carinthia, Carniola, Istria, Trieste, Gorizia and Gradisca and which in the 16th and 17th centuries were independent counties.

The town came into its own under the

Sog. Gottesplagenbild, Fresko von
Thomas von Villach, 1480, Reproduktion

God's Plagues, fresco by
Thomas von Villach, 1480, reproduction

Die erste Blütezeit der Stadt begann mit Kaiser Friedrich III. von Habsburg (1453–1493), der sich hier bevorzugt aufhielt und der Stadt nicht nur viele Privilegien gewährte, sondern auch das Stadtbild durch hervorragende Bauten bereicherte.
So ließ er an der Ostecke der Stadt ab 1438 eine Stadtburg erbauen (heutige Burg), die als Residenz des Kaisers diente (siehe Stadtkrone) und der Burg gegenüber gleichzeitig den gotischen Neubau der Ägydiuskirche (heutige Grazer Dom, 1438–1462) errichten.
In der Murvorstadt wurde die Bürgerspitalskirche (ab 2. Hälfte 15. Jahrhundert) und in der nun auch nach Süden geöffneten Stadt (Eisernes Tor) das Dominikanerkloster (heute Stadtpfarrkirche) errichtet. Im Norden kam das zweite Sackviertel hinzu.
Harte kriegerische Auseinandersetzungen waren mit den Ungarn und den Türken zu führen. Die mittelalterlichen Stadtbefestigungen

Habsburg emperor Frederick III (1453–93), who made Graz his favourite residence. He granted the town many privileges and enriched the townscape with an abundance of magnificent buildings.
From 1438 onwards, he had a town castle built at the eastern corner of the town (today's Burg), which served as the emperor's residence (see "Stadtkrone"), and he ordered the rebuilding of the church of St Ägydius in the new Gothic style (today's cathedral, 1438–1462).
In the Mur village, construction of the Burghers' Hospice Church was begun in the second half of the 15th century. The town had at last opened up to the south (Iron Gate), where the Dominican Monastery (today's Parish Church) was built. The second Sack quarter developed in the north.
Town and country became involved in serious armed conflicts with the Hungarians and the

IV

Landhaus, Arkadenhof
Landhaus, arcaded courtyard

IV

wurden verstärkt, 1480 kamen die Türken bis vor die Stadt; das Gottesplagenbild, eines der ursprünglich qualitätsvollsten gotischen Fresken an der Südwand des Grazer Domes, gemalt vom Meister Thomas von Villach, hat diese Geschehnisse festgehalten.

Kaiser Maximilian, Sohn Friedrichs III., hielt sich nur selten in Graz auf, baute aber am Burgkomplex weiter (Doppelwendeltreppe 1499, siehe Stadtkrone).

Das 16. Jahrhundert wird durch ein weiteres Vordringen der Türken, das Eindringen der Reformation (ab 1525) und durch zunehmenden wirtschaftlichen Niedergang bestimmt.

Als Gegenmaßnahme wurde unter König Ferdinand I. von Habsburg nach 1543 das gesamte mittelalterliche Befestigungssystem der Stadt durch lombardische Architekten und Handwerker nach den modernsten Erkenntnissen der Festungsbaukunst zur „Hauptfestung Innerösterreichs" umgestaltet.

Zu dieser Zeit erhielt die Stadt die Charakteristika einer Renaissancebefestigung mit breiten vorgeschobenen Bastionen. Zudem wurde das alte Hochschloss auf dem Schlossberg abgetragen und durch einen Neubau ersetzt (heutige Kasematten). Auch das Wahrzeichen der Stadt, der Uhrturm (kürzlich wurden ältere Substruktionen aus gotischer Zeit entdeckt), erhielt um 1559 sein charakteristisches, heute noch bestehendes Aussehen. Die Oberleitung dieser Arbeiten hatte Domenico dell'Aglio aus Lugano inne. Dieser errichtete auch für die steirischen Landstände (steirische Regierung) von 1557 bis 1565 den bedeutendsten Renaissancebau des Landes, das sog. Landhaus.

Turks. As a result, the medieval fortifications were reinforced. In 1480 the Turks arrived at the town-gates. These events are captured in a fresco entitled "God's Plagues" on the southern wall of the cathedral, painted by Master Thomas von Villach which ranks among the highest-quality frescoes of the Gothic period.

Emperor Maximilian, the son of Frederick III, spent very little time in Graz but continued to add annexes to the Burg complex (double spiral staircase in 1499, see "Stadtkrone").

The 16th century was dominated by the constant threat of a Turkish invasion, the advance of the Reformation (from 1525 onwards), and by a gradually accelerating economic decline.

As a countermeasure, after 1543 King Ferdinand I of Habsburg called in architects and craftsmen from Lombardy to rebuild and renew the entire medieval system of fortifications in line with state-of-the-art fortress design, turning the town into the "main stronghold of Inner Austria".

At that time the town acquired the characteristic features of a Renaissance fortress with broad bastions advancing across the entire line of defence. The old castle on the Schlossberg was pulled down and replaced by a new building (today's casemates). In c. 1559, the Clock Tower, landmark of Graz, received the characteristic appearance that has been preserved to this day (older substructures from the Gothic period were discovered only recently). The works were supervised by Domenico dell'Aglio from Lugano, who also constructed the most important Styrian Renaissance building, the Landhaus (1557–65) for the Styrian estates (Styrian diet).

IV

Hofgasse 10, ehem. Jesuitengymnasium, sog. Taubenkobel, Hofansicht

Hofgasse 10, former Jesuit college, dovecot, view of the courtyard

Graz als Residenz von Innerösterreich

Eine weitere habsburgische Länderteilung unter den Söhnen Ferdinands I. machte Graz 1564 neuerlich zur Hauptstadt des innerösterreichischen Länderverbandes, der nun von den Alpen bis zur Adria reichte und der auch für die Sicherung der Militärgrenze verantwortlich war.

Die wichtigste Zeit für die Grazer städtebauliche Entwicklung ist zweifelsohne unter dem Landesfürsten Erzherzog Karl II. von Innerösterreich (1564–1590) und dessen Gattin Maria von Bayern sowie deren Sohn Ferdinand anzusehen. Diese unterhielten hier eine eigene Hofhaltung, schufen neue Regierungsbehörden und verhalfen der Stadt zu einer neuen kulturellen und geistigen Blütezeit.

Politisch waren es die Abwehrmaßnahmen gegen die Türken und die Auseinandersetzungen zwischen dem katholischen Landesfürsten und den in der Mehrzahl evangelischen Ständen, welche die Szene beherrschten. Letztere versuchten über ihr Steuerbewilligungsrecht ihre Religionsfreiheit zu sichern.

1568 waren etwa drei Viertel der Grazer Bevölkerung protestantisch. Es wurde die sog. protestantische Stiftsschule errichtet (Paradeishof, heute Kaufhaus Kastner und Öhler); an dieser Schule wirkten hervorragende Männer des evangelischen Deutschlands, darunter von 1594 bis 1598 der Astronom und Mathematiker Johannes Kepler und der protestantische Theologe David Chyträus.

Der wichtigste Abschnitt in der städtebaulichen Entwicklung war die Berufung der Jesuiten 1572 nach Graz. Durch die große Förderung des Jesuitenordens leitete Erzherzog Karl II. damit die Gegenreformation ein.

Graz – Capital of Inner Austria

Another partition of the Habsburg lands among the sons of Ferdinand I in 1564 made Graz once again the capital of Inner Austria, an association of territories that now extended from the Alps to the Adriatic Sea and was charged with guarding the military frontier against the Turks.

Without doubt the most important period of urban development occurred under Archduke Charles II of Inner Austria (1564–90) and his wife, Maria of Bavaria, and their son Ferdinand. They maintained a complete household in Graz, created new administrative authorities and helped the town to achieve a new cultural and intellectual heyday.

The political scene was dominated by the defensive measures against the Turks and conflicts between the Catholic prince and the predominantly Protestant estates. The latter tried to use their tax granting privileges in order to secure religious freedom.

In 1568 about three quarters of the population of Graz were Protestants. They maintained the Protestant foundation school (Paradeishof, today the department store Kastner und Öhler) where several distinguished men from Protestant Germany taught, among them (from 1594 to 1598) Johannes Kepler, astronomer and mathematician, and the Protestant theologian David Chyträus.

The most important chapter of urban development began when the Jesuits were called to Graz in 1572. By patronising the Jesuit Order, Archduke Charles II prepared the way for the Counter-Reformation in Graz.

The Order took over the grammar school in Hofgasse, built the Jesuit College (today's Seminary, Bürgergasse) next to the court residence, and was given the parish church

Der Orden übernahm zuerst das Gymnasium in der Hofgasse, erbaute sich in der Nähe der Burg-Anlage das Jesuitenkollegium (heute Priesterseminar, Bürgergasse) und erhielt die Stadtpfarre St. Ägydius (Grazer Dom) übertragen. Damals übersiedelte die Stadtpfarre ins ehemalige Dominikanerkloster in der Herrengasse (heute Stadtpfarrkirche).

Von 1580 bis 1621 war Graz auch Sitz einer ständigen päpstlichen Nuntiatur. Nach 1582 verschärfte sich der Druck auf die protestantische Bürgerschaft.

Die Gründung der Jesuiten-Universität 1585 durch Erzherzog Karl geschah nicht zuletzt als katholische Reaktion auf den Erfolg der protestantischen Stiftsschule.

Den vorzüglichen Lehrern aus dem Jesuitenorden gelang es rasch, die Universität zu einem geistigen Ausstrahlungspunkt über Innerösterreich hinaus für den pannonischen und den Karpatenraum zu machen.

Diese Maßnahmen waren bald von Erfolg gekrönt, denn Karls Sohn vollendete die Rekatholisierung von Graz. Die protestantische Stiftsschule musste geschlossen werden, und im Jahr 1600 wurden die evangelischen Bürger sowie 1628 die Adeligen ausgewiesen.

Die Gegenreformation hatte jedoch eine gewaltige Bauentwicklung in der Stadt bewirkt; neue Kirchen und Klöster wurden errichtet.

So entstanden vor dem Paulustor ab 1600 das Kapuzinerkloster mit der Antoniuskirche. Unmittelbar davor verbrannten die Jesuiten auf demselben Platz mit großem propagandistischem Aufwand etwa 10.000 protestantische Bücher, allerdings nur die Doppelstücke, die Erstausgaben blieben wohlverwahrt in der Universitätsbibliothek.

Ab 1615 ließ sich Erzherzog Ferdinand durch den Hofkünstler Pietro de Pomis neben der Hofkirche sein monumentales Mausoleum

of St. Ägydius (cathedral). The municipal parish was moved to the former Dominican monastery in Herrengasse (today's Parish Church). In addition, Graz was the seat of a permanent papal legate from 1580 until 1621. As a consequence of their activities pressure on the Protestant burghers began to increase noticeably after 1582.

In 1585 Archduke Charles founded the Jesuit University, not least as a Catholic reaction to the success of the Protestant foundation school. Owing to excellent teachers from the Jesuit Order the university soon became an intellectual focus, its influence reaching far beyond the borders of Inner Austria into the Pannonian and Carpathian regions.

These measures soon reaped rewards: the Catholic restoration of Graz was completed under Charles' son. The Protestant foundation school was closed, and the Protestant burghers were expelled in 1600, a fate that befell the aristocratic estates likewise in 1628.

However, the Counter-Reformation had resulted in enormous building activities in the town, such as the construction of new churches and monasteries. The Capuchin Monastery and St. Anthony's Church were built outside the Paulus Gate. It was in front of this building that the Jesuits burnt about 10,000 Protestant books, accompanied by much publicity and propaganda; although what they actually burned were duplicates – the originals remained safely stowed away in the university library.

In 1615, Archduke Ferdinand commissioned his court artist Pietro de Pomis to build a monumental mausoleum adjacent to the court church, which became the largest and most impressive Habsburg mausoleum in Austria, as well as the country's most important historical building from the period of

IV

Grazer Dom
Mausoleum Kaiser Ferdinands II.

Cathedral
Mausoleum of Emperor Ferdinand II

errichten, der größte und beeindruckendste Mausoleumsbau der Habsburger in Österreich und bedeutendstes Baudenkmal Österreichs aus der Zeit der Übergangsphase des Manierismus zum Barock.

Eine weitere Zäsur in der Stadtentwicklung ergab sich durch die Wahl Erzherzog Ferdinands 1618 zum römisch-deutschen Kaiser. 1619 übersiedelte der Hof nach Wien und mit ihm verließen die Schatzkammer, die Hofmusikkapelle und die Lipizzaner die Stadt, und doch war es zunächst der Grazer Hof, der in Wien weiterlebte. Der Wegzug des Hofes aus Graz bedeutete für die Stadt einen allmählichen wirtschaftlichen und kulturellen Verlust. Diese Tatsache erklärt auch, warum sich Graz nicht zu einer Stadt des Hochbarock wandeln konnte, bis 1749 blieb Graz dennoch die Hauptstadt Innerösterreichs.

Das 17. Jahrhundert

Wie bereits erwähnt, wurden die Bauaufgaben zunächst durch die sog. „welschen" (italienischen) Meister getragen, wobei ab der zweiten Hälfte des 17. Jahrhunderts auch vermehrt wieder einheimische Künstler beauftragt wurden. 1656 kam in Graz der große Barockbaumeister Johann Bernhard Fischer von Erlach zur Welt.

Anstelle von mehreren Bürgerhäusern entstanden die Bauflächen für bedeutende Renaissance- und frühbarocke Adelspalais, so z. B. das Palais Kollonitsch, das Palais des Effans d' Avernas und das Palais Stubenberg, später Welsersheimb. Das Bürgertum versuchte diesen neuen Entwicklungen mit Fassadenneugestaltungen und dem Einbau von Arkadenhöfen in bestehende ältere Bausubstanz zu folgen.

Im Westen der Stadt wurde durch den inner-

transition from Mannerism to Baroque.

The election of Archduke Ferdinand as Holy Roman Emperor in 1618 marked another turning point in urban development. In 1619 the Court moved to Vienna, taking with it the treasury, the court orchestra and the Lipizzaner horses, yet for the time being it remained the Court of Graz living in Vienna. The departure of the Court from Graz triggered a gradual economic and cultural decline, and it also explains why the high Baroque style did not take hold in Graz. Graz nonetheless remained the capital of Inner Austria until 1749.

The 17th Century

As has already been mentioned, it was originally Italian (so-called "welsch") masters who carried out the construction works. From the second half of the 17th century onwards, however, local artists were increasingly commissioned. The great Baroque architect Johann Bernhard Fischer von Erlach was born in Graz, in 1656.

Several burgher houses made way for notable Renaissance and early Baroque palaces of the nobility, such as Palais Kollonitsch, Palais des Effans d'Avernas and Palais Stubenberg, later Welsersheimb. The burghers tried to emulate the new fashion by remodeling facades and adding arcaded courtyards to older buildings.

In the western part of the town the governor of Inner Austria, Hans Ulrich von Eggenberg, built a magnificent ducal residence in

IV

Landeszeughaus, Waffenkammer
Armoury, exhibition hall fitted as armoury

österreichischen Statthalter Hans Ulrich von Eggenberg in den Jahren 1625 bis 1656 eine prunkvolle Fürstenresidenz erbaut. Das Schloss Eggenberg mit seiner künstlerisch wertvollen Innenausstattung ist das bedeutendste Barockschloss der Steiermark.

Das ausklingende 17. Jahrhundert bringt für Graz ein neuerliches Aufflammen der Türkengefahr, eine weitere Gefährdung durch aufständische Ungarn und eine Pestkatastrophe bedrohlichen Ausmaßes, der 1680 etwa ein Viertel aller Grazer zum Opfer fiel. 1664 wurden die Türken in der Schlacht bei Mogersdorf-St. Gotthard durch Graf Montecuccoli geschlagen, wofür die dankbaren Grazer die Mariensäule am Eisernen Tor stifteten. Die Stadt verfügte über drei Rüsthäuser von denen das ständische Zeughaus in der Herrengasse als das vollständigste Waffenarsenal dieser Zeit noch erhalten ist. Es wurde 1643/44 von Antonio Solar erbaut, die Skulpturen beim Eingang stammen von Giovanni Mamolo. Im Inneren dienen vier, durch hölzerne Balkendecken unterteilte Stockwerksäle als Waffenkammern, und es ist heute eines der wenigen erhaltenen Zeughäuser Europas.

1673 heiratete Kaiser Leopold I. in der Hofkirche Claudia Felicitas von Tirol, wobei das Hochzeitsfest im Schloss Eggenberg abgehalten wurde.

1625–56. Eggenberg Palace, with its interior decoration of great artistic merit, is the most important Baroque palace in Styria.

In the late 17th century Graz was again confronted with the Turkish peril, aggravated by Hungarian insurgents and a plague epidemic of horrendous proportions, with a death toll in 1680 of about 25 % of the population. In 1664 the Turks were defeated by Count Montecuccoli in the battle of Mogersdorf–St. Gotthard, in commemoration of which feat the grateful inhabitants of Graz donated Our Lady's Column on Europaplatz.

The town owned three armouries; one of them, the Estate Armoury in Herrengasse, exists to this day as the most complete collection of weapons from that time. It was built in 1643/44 by Antonio Solar; the stone dressing work was carried out by Giovanni Mamolo. Inside, four storeys divided by wooden joist ceilings serve as display rooms for the collection which constitutes one of the few armouries still in existence in Europe.

In 1673 Emperor Leopold I married Claudia Felicitas of Tyrol in the court church, and the wedding celebrations took place at Eggenberg Palace.

Das 18. Jahrhundert

Das 18. Jahrhundert brachte für Graz ein endgültiges Erlöschen der Türkengefahr und damit ein Abrücken von den politischen Schauplätzen des großen Weltgeschehens.

Dafür erhielt die Stadt, veranlasst durch die merkantilistische Wirtschaftspolitik Karls VI., die Reichs-Commercialstraße Wien–Triest

The 18th Century

The 18th century finally saw the end of the Turkish peril for Graz. The town began to be sidelined from the stage of world politics.

However, under Charles VI and his mercantilist policy, Graz was made a stage of the Imperial Commercial Road from Vienna to Trieste, which gave the town a new outlook

IV

Palais Wildenstein
Palais Wildenstein

und damit eine wirtschaftliche Neuorientierung nach dem Süden und dem Südosten. Es entstanden Fabriken und erste Bankhäuser.
Durch die zentralistischen Reformen verlor der Magistrat den größten Teil seiner Selbständigkeit; die innerösterreichischen Behörden wurden aufgelöst.
In der Stadt wurden nur mehr wenige hervorragende Palaisbauten errichtet, wie z. B. das Palais Attems (ab 1702) und das Palais Wildenstein (1710/15), dagegen wurden bereits bestehende Wallfahrtsorte zu monumentalen Zentren ausgebaut. (Maria Hilf, Maria Trost).
Die einschneidenden Maßnahmen des Josefinismus hatten für Graz zur Folge, dass von sechzehn Klöstern neun geschlossen wurden und für die Stadt ein neues System von Pfarren eingerichtet werden musste. Gleichzeitig kamen die Bücherbestände von vierzig steirischen und Kärntner Klöstern nach Graz und

towards the south and south-east. Factories and the first banking houses appeared.
Centralising reforms deprived the magistrate of most of its independence; the Inner-Austrian authorities were dissolved.
In the town the number of outstanding new palaces (such as Palais Attems, from 1702 and Palais Wildenstein, 1710–15) dwindled, while existing places of pilgrimage were developed into monumental shrines (Maria Hilf, Maria Trost).
The suppression of the convents undertaken by Joseph II led to the closing of nine out of 16 monasteries and to a new system of parishes in Graz. At the same time, books from 40 Styrian and Carinthian monasteries were brought to Graz, enlarging the stocks of the university library.
In 1786 the Bishop of Seckau moved his residence to Graz, the church of St. Ägydius be-

IV

Schlossbergbombardement, 1809,
Stadtmuseum Graz

Bombardment of the Schlossberg, 1809,
Graz City Museum

bereicherten die Bestände der Grazer Universitätsbibliothek.

1786 übersiedelte der Bischof von Seckau nach Graz, der Grazer Dom wurde Bischofskirche und die Diözese Graz-Seckau gegründet. Der Jesuitenorden wurde bereits 1773 aufgehoben und die Universität in ein staatliches Lyceum umgestaltet.

1784 wurde durch ein allmähliches Aufheben der Befestigungsanlagen die Verschmelzung der Altstadt mit der Vorstädten vorbereitet. Südlich des Eisernen Tores entstand durch Caspar Andreas v. Jakomini die später nach ihm benannte Jakominivorstadt.

Die sich anbahnende günstige wirtschaftliche Entwicklung wurde durch die Koalitionskriege mit Frankreich empfindlich gestört. Die Franzosen besetzten dreimal die Stadt, 1797 (Aufenthalt Napoleons in der Stadt), 1805 und 1809 und forderten harte Kontributionen von

came a cathedral, and the diocese of Graz–Seckau was founded. The Jesuit order had been dissolved in 1773, and its university was converted into a state university.

From 1784 onwards the fortifications were gradually demolished, so that the historic center began to merge with the adjacent villages. To the south of the Iron Gate, Caspar Andreas von Jakomini built the suburb which was later to bear his name.

The beginnings of favourable economic development were considerably impeded by the Wars of the Coalitions against France. The French occupied Graz three times, in 1797 (when Napoleon stayed in the town), 1805, and 1809, and demanded exorbitant contributions from its inhabitants. In 1809 they laid siege to the Schlossberg, without much success thanks to a brave defence led by Major Hackher. Under the provisions of the Peace

IV

Stadtparkbrunnen
Fountain in the City Park

der Stadt. 1809 wurde der Schlossberg durch die Franzosen belagert, doch konnten diese gegen die tapfere Verteidigung Major Hackhers wenig ausrichten. Dennoch mussten die Befestigungsanlagen nach den Bestimmungen des Schönbrunner Friedens geschleift werden. Ab 1839 wurde der kahle Schlossbergfelsen durch Freiherr von Welden in die für das Stadtbild so charakteristische Parkanlage umgestaltet.

In die Periode des Vormärz fällt auch das vielfältige Wirken Erzherzog Johanns († 1859), der die Grundlagen für heute noch wirksame kulturelle und wirschaftliche Institutionen legte (Joanneum, Landesarchiv und -bibliothek, Technische Universität, Landwirtschafts-, Versicherungs- und Sparkassenwesen etc.).

Das Revolutionsjahr von 1848 gestaltete sich für Graz gemäßigter. Das deutsch-national gesinnte Bürgertum übernahm bis 1918 die Führung. Zu dieser Zeit war Graz als Pensionistenstadt beliebt und zahlreiche Musiker und Schriftsteller lebten hier (Robert Hamerling, Peter Rosegger, Wilhelm Kienzl, Hugo Wolf).

Auf dem kommunalen Sektor brachte diese Periode zahlreiche Maßnahmen, die zu einer modernen Urbanität führten. So wurden die militärischen Glacisgründe für die Schaffung des Stadtparkes angekauft, die Bezirks- und Gasseneinteilung vorgenommen, Häusernummerierung, die Regulierung von Stadtvierteln mittels Bebauungsplänen. Die städtebauliche Entscheidung, das Glacis nicht zu verbauen, ermöglichte die Anlegung des Stadtparkes, dadurch blieb die Altstadt quasi konservierend erhalten, historische Monumentalbauten entstanden in den Stadterweiterungsvierteln. Die im Biedermeier einsetzende Stadterweiterung intensivierte sich in der sogenannten Gründerzeit. Stadtplane-

of Schönbrunn, however, the fortifications were pulled down. From 1839 onwards, a park was laid out on the barren Schlossberg rock by Baron von Welden, giving the townscape a special appeal which has lasted ever since. The prerevolutionary Vormärz period is also characterised by the diverse activities of Archduke John (died in 1859), who laid the foundations for several cultural and economic institutions still active today (Joanneum, Styrian archives and library, Technical University, agricultural and insurance institutions, savings banks, etc.)

The 1848 revolution turned out to be a moderate affair in Graz. The middle classes, predominantly of German-nationalistic convictions, took over until 1918. At that time Graz enjoyed popularity among pensioners, attracting many musicians and writers, such as Robert Hamerling, Peter Rosegger, Wilhelm Kienzl and Hugo Wolf.

For the municipality, this was a period of changes working towards modern urbanity. The city purchased the sites of the military glacis in order to create the city park, developed district and street plans, numbered the houses, and regulated the development of new quarters by zoning ordinances. The decision not to build on the glacis made it possible to create the city park, and at the same time preserved the historic center more or less in its original state, while grand Historicist buildings sprang up in the new urban enlargement areas. The urban extension which began in the Biedermeier period intensified in the "Gründerzeit" (boom time). Urban planning concepts could be put into effect in the grid building system; green policy found its expression in the creation of the city park on the glacis sites of the Volksgarten in the Mur village and of the Augarten in the southern extension area.

IV

Hauptplatz mit Rathaus
Hauptplatz, city hall

rische Konzepte wurden in der Rasterverbauung fassbar, Grünpolitik in der Anlage des Stadtparks auf den Glacisgründen, des Volksgartens, in der Murvorstadt und des Augartens im südlichen Stadterweiterungsgebiet.

Die innere Stadt wurde zur City. Wichtige historistische Großbauten entstanden, wie das Rathaus (1888 bis 1893), die technische Universität, die Karl-Franzens-Universität (1885) , das Stadttheater (Oper), die neugotische Herz-Jesu-Kirche, die Synagoge, Banken, Hotels sowie das Landeskrankenhaus, eine monumentale, großzügige Anlage in Jugendstilformen, die bei ihrer Eröffnung 1912 als „Weltwunder" galt.

Die Ermordung des im Grazer Palais Khuenburg (heute Stadtmuseum) geborenen Thronfolgers Erzherzog Franz Ferdinand gab den unmittelbaren Anlass für den Ausbruch des 1. Weltkrieges. Mit den neuen 1918/19 gezogenen Grenzen verlor Graz sein Hinterland und wurde damit in ein wirtschaftliches und verkehrspolitisches Abseits gedrängt.

Nach dem 2. Weltkrieg setzte eine Periode langsamer Normalisierung ein. 1938 wurden die umliegenden Gemeinden, insgesamt 17 Bezirke zum heutigen Großraum Graz zusammengefasst. Die Entwicklung zur modernen Großstadt, zur Industrie-, Kultur-, Universitäts- und Gartenstadt nahm ihren Lauf.

So machen neben der einzigartigen Altstadt, die Straßenzüge und Stadtviertel mit bedeutenden Bauten des Historismus, des Jugendstiles und der Modernen Architektur Graz zu einer lebendigen Architekturausstellung.

The inner city became the commercial and social center of Graz. Important Historicist structures were built, such as the City Hall (1888–93), the Technical University, Karl-Franzens University (1885), the City Theatre (opera), the neo-Gothic Herz-Jesu-Kirche, the synagogue, banks, hotels, and the Provincial Hospital, a monumental assembly with Jugendstil elements considered a "wonder of the world" when it opened in 1912.

The assassination of the successor to the imperial throne, Archduke Franz Ferdinand, who had been born in Graz in Palais Khuenburg (today's City Museum), provided the spark for the outbreak of the First World War. With the new Austrian borders drawn in 1918/19, Graz lost its hinterland and was relegated to the background economically as well as geographically.

After the Second World War, a period of slow normalisation set in. The surrounding municipalities, 17 districts in all, had been united into today's Greater Graz by 1938. Graz became a modern city, an industrial and cultural center, a city of universities and gardens.

Today, the unique historic center and the newer streets and areas with their outstanding buildings of Historicism, Jugendstil and modern architecture combine to make Graz a living showpiece of the art of architecture.

Center am Kai, Sackstraße
Center am Kai, Sackstraße

IV

Sog. Florentiner Ansicht von Graz, aquarellierte Federzeichnung um 1565
"Florentine View" of Graz, pen-and-ink drawing, painted in watercolours, c. 1565

IV

Städtebauliche Entwicklung von Graz

Das mittelalterliche Stadtbild

Geschichtlich fassbar wird Graz am Anfang des 12. Jahrhunderts. Grundherr des Grazer Bodens war Bernhard von Stübing, der nach 1122 die unbesiedelte Auenlandschaft mit Dörfern besetzte (in der Chronik des Stiftes Rein findet man die urkundlich älteste schriftliche Nennung von Graz aus dem Jahre 1128). Die slawische Bezeichnung gradec (= kleine Burg), von der sich der Name der Stadt Graz ableitet, weist auf die ursprüngliche Aufgabe dieses Ortes hin: Schutz und Zuflucht zu bieten.

Die entscheidende Entwicklung für Graz brachte die 2. Hälfte des 12. Jahrhunderts. 1156 erwarb der Traungauer Otakar III. den Grazer Boden. Die Markgrafen von Steyr (Steiermark), das Geschlecht der Traungauer machten in der Folge die Stadt zum Mittelpunkt des Handels und der Landesverwaltung in der Steiermark. Zwischen 1130 und 1140 entstand der erste Gassenmarkt als planmäßige mittelalterliche Marktanlage zwischen Hauptplatz und Schlossbergplatz, senkrecht zur alten Durchzugsstraße im Schutze des Burgberges, danach die Neugründung des Marktplatzes und die Anlegung von Herrengasse und Schmiedgasse.

Graz zeigt sich als kleine aber aufstrebende Siedlung am südlichen und westlichen Abhang des Schlossberges mit der gegen Osten gelegenene Pfarrkirche, die dem hl. Ägydius geweiht war (später Domkirche von Graz). Der hl. Ägydius ist der Schutzpatron der Reisenden, ein Hinweis auf eine alte Römerstraße, die von Osten kommend, über eine Murfurt an die Nord-Süd verlaufende Römerstraße im Westen des Grazer Beckens an-

The Urban Development of Graz

The Medieval Town

History first takes notice of Graz at the beginning of the 12th century. After 1122 the landowner Bernhard von Stübing began to clear the river forest and establish villages (in the chronicle of Rein Abbey, Graz is first mentioned in a deed dated 1128). The Slavic name gradec (=small fortress), from which the name of Graz is derived, indicates the original function of the place, i.e. to provide protection and refuge.

The second half of the 12th century was decisive for the development of Graz. In 1156 Otakar III of Traungau acquired the land of Graz. The Traungau dynasty, the margraves of Steyer (Styria), made Graz the centre of commerce and trade as well as the seat of the Styrian administration. Between 1130 and 1140 the first street market evolved as a planned medieval market complex between Hauptplatz and Schlossbergplatz, at right angles to the old highway, protected by the Burg hill. It was later replaced by a new market square, built together with Herrengasse and Schmiedgasse.

Graz was by now a small but promising settlement at the southern and western inclines of the Schlossberg, with the parish church – dedicated to St. Ägydius (later Graz Cathedral) – situated towards the east. St. Ägydius is the patron saint of travellers, who may have already watched the old Roman road that came from the east and continued through a Mur ford, in the west of the Grazer Feld joining another Roman road that ran from north to south (along what is now Hofgasse and Sporgasse over the Mur bridge). Otakar IV, seriously ill and without an heir,

IV

Hauptplatz mit ältesten Straßenzügen
(Sporgasse, Sackstraße), Luftaufnahme 1991

Hauptplatz and oldest remaining streets
(Sporgasse, Sackstrasse), aerial photograph, 1991

schloss (Verlauf der heutigen Hofgasse und Sporgasse über die Murbrücke).

Der kinderlose, schwerkranke Otakar IV. wurde 1180 als erster und zugleich letzter Traungauer zum Herzog ernannt; in der berühmten Georgenberger Handfeste (1186) sicherte er dem Babenberger Leopold V. die Herrschaft in der Steiermark und damit diesem Land die Zugehörigkeit zu Österreich.

Die Babenberger förderten die rasche urbane Entwicklung. Nach dem Aussterben dieses Geschlechtes sollten die Habsburger (mit Rudolf I., 1282 beginnend) fast 650 Jahre lang das Schicksal dieser Stadt bestimmen.

Im Neuberger Vertrag von 1379 teilten sich die Brüder Albrecht III. und Leopold III. die habsburgischen Länder, wodurch die Grundlage für ein selbständiges innerösterreichisches Territorium mit Steiermark, Kärnten, Krain und Istrien gegeben war.

was the first and last of the Traungau dynasty on whom the title of duke was bestowed. In the famous "Georgenberg Treaty of Inheritance" (1186) he appointed the Babenberg Duke Leopold V as his successor in Styria, thus bringing Styria into Austria.

The Babenbergs encouraged the town's rapid development. When their dynasty became extinct, the Habsburgs (beginning with Rudolf I, 1282) were to determine the fate of Graz for almost 650 years.

In the 1379 Treaty of Neuberg the brothers Albrecht III and Leopold III divided the Habsburg lands between themselves, creating the basis for an independent Inner Austrian territory that comprised Styria, Carinthia, Carniola and Istria.

Graz became the capital of Leopold and his successors. Its first period as the seat of the court was overshadowed by discord among

IV

Burg mit Stadttor
Burg and town gate

Graz wurde zur Residenzstadt der Leopoldinischen Linie der Habsburger. Die erste Phase als Residenzstadt war durch Zwistigkeiten unter den Habsburgern geprägt. Erst durch die Übernahme der Regierung Innerösterreichs durch Herzog Friedrich, dem späteren Kaiser Friedrich III., setzte ab 1435 ein baulicher Aufschwung der Stadt ein. Friedrich begünstigte Graz und förderte eine Reihe kirchlicher und profaner Bauten. (Die starke Verschuldung der Bürger an die Juden gab 1438/39 den Anlass zu deren Vertreibung und zur Auflösung des Ghettos im südlichen Herrengassenbereich. In den folgenden Jahren wurden die Judenhäuser an die Grazer Bürger verkauft.)

Die entscheidendste städtebauliche Tat war der Bau einer neuen Residenz, einer Stadtburg auf dem Areal des ehem. landesfürstlichen Meierhofes, wofür auch bürgerliche Häuser angekauft wurden, sowie der Neubau der alten Pfarrkirche St. Ägydius, die Friedrich durch einen Gang über der Hofgasse mit der Burg verbinden ließ.

Mit Stadtburg und gotischer Pfarrkirche (heute Dom) schuf Friedrich die Basis für die sog. Stadtkrone, einem einzigartigen Bauensemble mitteleuropäischer Sakralbaukunst (siehe Stadtkrone).

Zusammenfassend sei für das Ende des Mittelalters im ausgehenden 15. Jahrhundert festgehalten: Die im Frühmittelalter vorwiegend wirtschaftliche Bedeutung der Stadt bzw. Marktanlage kommt dadurch zum Ausdruck, dass Graz kein innerstädtisches Kirchenzentrum besaß. Die Paulskirche (heute Stiegenkirche) und die Ägidiuskirche hatten keinen nennenswerten Einfluss auf die Stadtentwicklung.

Dennoch besaß Graz zu diesem Zeitpunkt die entscheidenden qualitativen Kriterien für ihre Urbanität: Die Burg als Herrschaftssitz, die von the Habsburgs. It was only when Duke Frederick, the future Emperor Frederick III, came to the throne of Inner Austria in 1435 that a boom in construction began. Frederick favoured Graz and supported the building of several ecclesiastical and secular structures. Burghers at that time were heavily in debt to the Jews, which prompted their expulsion in 1438/39 and the dissolution of the ghetto, which was located in the southern precincts of Herrengasse. In the following years, the Jews' houses were sold to the burghers of Graz.

Frederick's urban planning activities culminated in the building of a new residence, a town castle, on the site of his former agricultural estate which was expanded by the purchase of several burgher houses. He also ordered the rebuilding of the old parish church of St. Ägydius and had it linked with his residence via a passage above Hofgasse. The town castle and Gothic parish church (today's cathedral) formed the nucleus of the so-called Stadtkrone, a building ensemble that is unique in Central European ecclesiastical architecture (see "Stadtkrone").

To conclude: in the early to late Middle Ages the town and market were primarily of economic importance, reflected by the fact that Graz had no ecclesiastical centre within its town walls. The churches of St. Paul (today's Stiegenkirche) and St. Ägydius had no appreciable influence on urban development. Nevertheless, Graz already possessed the qualitative criteria that determined its urbanity: the Burg as the prince's residence, the market complex surrounded by a ring wall, and the church of St. Ägydius as its ecclesiastical centre.

Typologically, Graz was a farming town, i.e. the majority of inhabitants were engaged in agriculture in addition to their trades. This is

IV

Sporgasse/Hofgasse, mittelalterliche Hofstätten-Anlage, Dachlandschaft

Sporgasse/Hofgasse, medieval homestead buildings, rooftops

einer Ringmauer umgebene Marktanlage, und als kirchliches Zentrum diente die Ägydiuskirche.

Graz gehörte zum Typus der Ackerbürgerstädte, d. h. ein Großteil der Bürger betrieb Landwirtschaft neben dem Gewerbe. Nachvollziehbar ist dies noch heute durch die Hofstätten-Anlage. Eine langgezogene Haus- und Hofform, die aus einem straßenseitigen Vorderhaus und einem Hinterhaus besteht (auch Stöckl), wobei Vorder- und Hinterhaus im Hofraum meist durch ein schmales Mittelhaus mit Gängen verbunden wird. Das Grazer Stadtbild dürfte sich im Frühmittelalter wenig von einer ländlichen Siedlung unterschieden haben, bis ins 15. Jahrhundert blieben auch einzelne Hofstätten unverbaut als Gartengrund.

Die langen Hofstätten sind am deutlichsten in der Häuserreihe vom Reinerhof in der Sackstraße, Sporgasse bis zur Stempfergasse erhalten und zählen zur ältesten und wertvollsten Bausubstanz der historischen Altstadt. In ihrer Geschlossenheit und homogenen Dachlandschaft (sog. Grabendächer) dokumentieren sie ein einzigartiges Zeugnis der Verbindung von Ackerbau und Bürgerschaft einer mittelalterlichen Gesellschaftsform.

evident to this day from a prevalence of so-called homestead buildings – a stretched-out form of house-cum-farmstead consisting of a front building facing the street and a rear building ("Stöckl"), usually connected in the courtyard by a narrow central building with corridors. The townscape of Graz in the early Middle Ages was probably not much different from a rural settlement. Several homestead courtyards were not built up but used as gardens up until the 15th century.

The long homestead buildings are best preserved in the row of houses from the Reinerhof in Sackstrasse to Stempfergasse; they number among the oldest and most valuable building stock of the historic center. With their self-contained design and homogenous roofscape featuring a succession of steep roofs, they testify to a unique co-existence of urban and rural life in a medieval society.

Spätgotik und Beginn der Renaissance

1493 verstarb Kaiser Friedrich III. Unter seinem Sohn und Nachfolger Kaiser Maximilian I. verlor Graz die Bedeutung einer Residenzstadt, da Maximilian im Gegensatz zu seinem Vater die Stadt selten besuchte. Die Zeit bis zum Tode Maximilians (1519) war von Bauernaufständen und einem allgemeinen Sittenverfall des Klerus geprägt, die den Nährboden für die nachfolgende Reforma-

Late Gothic and Early Renaissance

Emperor Frederick III died in 1493. Under his son and successor Emperor Maximilian I, Graz lost its standing as residence of the court, since Maximilian – unlike his father – rarely visited the town. The period until Maximilian's death (1519) was characterised by peasants' revolts and a general moral decline of the clergy that formed the breeding ground for the subsequent period of Reformation.

Ehem. Deutschordenshaus, spätgotischer Arkadeninnenhof, Sporgasse 22

Former house of the Teutonic Order, arcaded courtyard, Sporgasse 22

tionszeit bildeten.

Aus der Zeit der spätgotischen Profanbaukunst besitzt Graz ein einzigartiges weltberühmtes Kunstwerk. Der unter Maximilian errichtete Treppenturm in der Grazer Burg beherbergt die Doppelwendeltreppe, die mit ihren gegenläufig gedrehten Steinstiegen ein architektonisches Meisterwerk des Spätmittelalters im europäischen Raum darstellt (siehe Stadtkrone).

Weitere Beispiele besonders qualitativer Profanbaukunst haben sich in den Höfen von Sporgasse 22 (sog. Deutschordenshof) und Hauptplatz 15 erhalten.

Mit dem Tode Kaiser Maximilians ging eine Epoche zu Ende. Kaiser Karl V., der Enkel und Nachfolger Maximilians, überließ am Wormser Reichstag 1521 die österreichischen Länder seinem Bruder Ferdinand.

Die erste Zeit Ferdinands war gekennzeich-

Late Gothic secular architecture has left Graz a unique and world-famous work of art. The stairwell that Maximilian had built in the Burg houses the double-spiral staircase, whose dog-legged stone steps represent an architectural masterpiece of the late Middle Ages unparalleled in the German-speaking world (see "Stadtkrone").

Further examples of high-quality secular architecture are to be found in the courtyards of Sporgasse 22 (so-called house of the Teutonic Order) and Hauptplatz 15.

The death of Emperor Maximilian spelt the end of an epoch. Emperor Charles V, Maximilian's grandson and successor, ceded the Austrian territories to his brother Ferdinand at the Imperial Diet of Worms in 1521.

Ferdinand's first years were characterised by wars against the peasants and the Turks, as well as by the advance of Protestantism into

IV

Landhaushof
Landhaus, courtyard

net von Bauern- und Türkenkriegen und vom Eindringen des Protestantismus in die Steiermark. Obwohl Ferdinand ein Verbot der lutherischen Schriften erlassen hatte, kann Graz Mitte des 16. Jahrhunderts als eine protestantische Stadt angesehen werden.

Zur Bekämpfung der ständigen Türkengefahr beschloss Ferdinand, dass Graz ab 1544 zu einer der modernsten Waffentechnik angepassten Hauptfestung im innerösterreichischen Raum ausgebaut werden sollte. Zu diesem Zweck berief er den italienischen Baumeister Domenico dell'Aglio als obersten Bauleiter der Befestigungsanlagen nach Graz.

Mit dem Eintreffen italienischer Bauleute in Graz war der Übergang vom Mittelalter zur Neuzeit gegeben, der sich in der Baukunst ab dem 2. Viertel des 16. Jahrhunderts bis in das 18. Jahrhundert widerspiegeln sollte. Diese Frührenaissanceformen hatten also schon im 2. Viertel des 16. Jahrhunderts in Graz ihren Einzug gehalten, als Domenico dell'Aglio 1555 von den Landständen den Auftrag erhielt, den herrengassenseitigen Trakt des Landhauses zu erneuern.

Der vom Palasttypus Venetiens beeinflusste Landhausbau stellt den bedeutendsten Frührenaissancebau der Steiermark dar. Seine dominante oberitalienische Hauptfassade mit der charakteristischen Portalachse sowie der großzügige Landhaushof mit seinen hofseitigen Pfeilerarkaden heben das Landhaus weit über seine regionale Bedeutung hinaus.

Styria. Although Ferdinand had prohibited the spreading of Luther's writings, Graz had practically become a Protestant town by the middle of the 16th century.

To combat the constant Turkish peril, Ferdinand decided to develop Graz into a major stronghold of Inner Austria (as from 1544), in keeping with the latest achievements of weapon technology. For this purpose he invited the Italian master builder Domenico dell' Aglio to Graz in order to supervise the construction works on the fortifications.

The arrival of Italian craftsmen in Graz marked a transition from the Middle Ages to modern times that was to be reflected in architecture from the second quarter of the 16th century until the 18th century.

Early Renaissance forms had already made their appearance in Graz early in the second quarter of the 16th century when in 1555 Domenico dell'Aglio was commissioned by the Styrian estates to renovate the wing of the Landhaus facing Herrengasse.

The Landhaus building, influenced by a type of palace originating in Venetia, is the most important early Renaissance building in Styria. Thanks to its impressive Upper-Italian main facade with characteristic portal axis and its spacious courtyard with arcaded piers, the Landhaus is of far more than regional importance.

IV

Luftaufnahme Stadtkrone, Teilansicht
Stadtkrone, aerial view

Die Renaissance – Graz als Residenzstadt von Innerösterreich 1564–1619

Dieser Zeitraum stellt den wichtigsten Abschnitt in der Stadtgeschichte dar.
Das 16. Jahrhundert wurde bestimmt durch den Übertritt zahlreicher Adeliger und Bürger zur Lehre Luthers, durch die wirtschaftliche Notlage nach der Eroberung Ungarns, durch die Türken (die 1532 auch unmittelbar an Graz vorbeizogen) und durch den Ausbau der Stadt zur Hauptfestung Innerösterreichs.
Testamentarisch bestimmte Ferdinand I. die Teilung der österreichischen Erblande, sein jüngster Sohn Karl sollte Steiermark, Kärnten, Görz, Triest und das österreichische Istrien als Herrschaftsgebiet erhalten.
Ab 1564 residierte Erzherzog Karl als Landesfürst von Innerösterreich in Graz. In der Folge entstand hier eine landesfürstliche Zentralbehörde mit Hofkanzlei, Hofkammer und selbständigem innerösterreichischem Hofkriegsrat.
Karls Regierungsjahre waren von der Auseinandersetzung zwischen Protestanten und Katholiken beherrscht, wobei Karl und seine Gattin Maria von Bayern gemäß des Augsburger Religionsfriedens eine Rekatholisierung anstrebten.
Als Gegenzug zur evangelischen Stiftsschule, etwa neun Zehntel der Grazer Bürgerschaft waren evangelisch – berief Karl die Jesuiten, die 1572 ihre gegenreformatorische Lehrtätigkeit aufnahmen.
Der Zeitraum von 1564 bis 1619 bedeutete nicht nur geschichtlich, sondern auch baulich einen Höhepunkt in der Stadtentwicklung.
Mit dem Einzug Erzherzog Karls und den von Wien mitgekommenen Regierungsbeamten setzte eine umfangreiche landesfürstliche wie auch private Bautätigkeit ein. An der

The Renaissance – Graz as the Capital of Inner Austria 1564–1619

The Renaissance marked the most important period in the history of Graz. The 16th century was determined by the conversion of almost all nobles and burghers in the town to Lutheran teaching, the sufferings of the people when Hungary was conquered by the Turks (who almost entered Graz in 1532) and the development of the town into the main stronghold of Inner Austria.
In his will, Ferdinand I stipulated the partition of the Austrian lands; his youngest son, Charles, was to receive the territories of Styria, Carinthia, Gorizia, Trieste and the Austrian part of Istria. From 1564 onwards, Archduke Charles resided in Graz as the sovereign of Inner Austria. Subsequently this led to the establishment of a central authority with chancellery, court chamber and an independent Inner Austrian council of war.
Charles' rule was dominated by the conflict between Protestants and Catholics. He and his wife, Maria of Bavaria, strove to achieve a Catholic restoration in accordance with the terms of the Religious Peace of Augsburg.
As a countermove to the establishment of the Protestant foundation school (nine out of ten burghers of Graz were Protestants), Charles called in the Jesuits, who began their teaching activities in the spirit of the Counter-Reformation in 1572.
The period from 1564 to 1619 signified a peak in urban development, both historically and architecturally. The arrival of Archduke Charles and the government officials who had come with him from Vienna gave rise to extensive building activities, on the part of the sovereign as well as by private citizens. Construction work at the Burg continued almost without interruption under Archduke

IV

Äußeres Paulustor
Paulus Gate, exterior

Burg wurde unter Erzherzog Karl und bis zum Tode seiner Gattin Maria fast ununterbrochen gebaut.

In unmittelbarer Nähe zu Burg und Pfarrkirche entfalteten die Jesuiten ab 1572 ihren Machtbereich. Es wurden das Jesuitenkollegium (Priesterseminar) und die Alte Universität errichtet. Das Kollegium wurde unter der landesfürstlichen Patronanz durch Konvikt, Gymnasium und Ferdinandeum erweitert und 1607/09 durch den Bau einer Universität bekrönt (siehe Stadtkrone).

Durch den Ausbau nach dem italienischen Befestigungssystem erfolgte eine bedeutende Vergrößerung des Stadtgebietes. Diese betraf vor allem den Norden, wo durch die Anlegung von zwei Bastionen ein neuer Stadtteil – die Paulustorvorstadt – entstand. (siehe Paulustor).

Dieser sozusagen im Rücken der Burg angelegte Stadtteil ist nicht nur als Sicherung gegen die Türkengefahr, sondern auch gegen die protestantische Bürgerschaft zu werten, zumal in diesem Stadtteil nur katholische Hofbedienstete sowie Klöster eigene Grundstücke erhielten.

Nimmt man alle heute noch erhaltene Bausubstanz dieser Epoche – Monumental- und Jesuitenbauten, öffentliche und private Häuser und rechnet die heute noch in Resten bestehenden Befestigungsanlagen mit der neu angelegten Paulustorvorstadt dazu –, so ist zu ersehen, dass sich in der 2. Hälfte des 16. Jahrhunderts das Stadtgebiet nicht nur wesentlich vergrößert, sondern auch weitgehend erneuert hatte.

In einem Zeitraum von etwa vierzig Jahren war mehr als die Hälfte der Stadt eine einzige Baustelle, die eine auch für heutige Verhältnisse fast unvorstellbare Kapazität an Material und Arbeitskräften voraussetzte.

Eine Anzahl von Monumentalbauten aus die-

Charles until the death of his wife, Maria.

In the immediate vicinity of the Burg and parish church, the Jesuits began to expand their sphere of influence. They built the Jesuit college (Seminary) and the Old University. Under the sovereign's patronage the College was extended by the addition of a boarding and a grammar school, and the Ferdinandeum. In 1607–09, the complex was crowned by the building of a university (see "Stadtkrone").

As a result of the refortification in line with the Italian system of bastions, the municipal area was considerably enlarged. This above all focused on the north, where the construction of two bastions created a new part of the town – the Paulus Gate quarter.

This part of the town, located as it was at the back of the Burg, must be seen not only as intended for protection against the Turks, but also against the Protestant burghers, since only Catholic courtiers and monasteries were granted plots of land.

When we consider the stock of buildings still remaining from that period, i.e. monumental and Jesuit buildings, public and private houses, adding the fortifications (remnants of which still exist) and the newly established Paulus Gate quarter, it becomes obvious that in the second half of the 16th century the municipal area was undergoing extensive enlargement as well as renewal. For four decades more than half of the town was one large building site, which required material and manpower resources of an almost unimaginable scope even by today's standards.

A number of monumental buildings from that time have been preserved in their full Renaissance splendour, in particular the Burg structures and the Jesuit College (see "Stadtkrone").

In the historic center, about 50 galleried courtyards were created in that period,

ser Zeit sind in ihrem Renaissance-Erscheinungsbild intakt erhalten, hervorzuheben wären die Burgbauten und das Jesuitenkollegium (siehe Stadtkrone).

Im altstädtischen Bereich entstanden in dieser Zeit etwa 50 Innenhöfe mit Arkadengängen, die der Altstadt das Charakteristikum einer italienischen Renaissancestadt verleihen, eine Besonderheit, die städtebaulich im gesamten deutschen Sprachraum nirgendwo mehr anzutreffen ist.

Die Bauten der 2. Hälfte des 16. Jahrhunderts müssen in unmittelbarem Zusammenhang mit den für den Festungsbau nach Graz berufenen Baumeistern und Maurern zu sehen sein. Den Großteil der mittelalterlichen Stadt wird man sich aus Holz vorstellen müssen. Aus einem Bericht von 1531 geht hervor, dass selbst das Schloss auf dem Schlossberg „gar alt und hölzern war".

Gleichzeitig mit der Neubefestigung der Stadtmauer setzte sich nun im 16. Jahrhundert die Ziegelbauweise entscheidend durch. Für Schlosser, Tischler und Malerarbeiten wurden einheimische Handwerker herangezogen, als Maurer und Steinmetze fungierten fast ausschließlich „welsche" Bauleute.

Soweit dies nachvollziehbar ist, stammten die meisten Maurer- und Steinmetzfamilien überwiegend aus dem Gebiet zwischen Comer und Luganer See; von Como (Bertoletti) über das Val d´Intelvi (dell´Aglio, Ferrabosco) bis Lugano (della Porta de Pone) und dem kleinen Nachbardorf Gandria (die Familien der Tadei und de Verda).

Diese Bauleute werden allgemein als Comasken „maestri comacini" bezeichnet, eine Bezeichnung, die sich für die erste große Einwanderungswelle im 16. Jahrhundert eingebürgert hatte. Zum überwiegenden Teil wurden die aus diesem Gebiet in erster Linie für den Festungsbau aufgenommenen Baumei-

giving the historic center the appeal of an Italian Renaissance town, a feature not found anywhere else in the entire German-speaking world.

The buildings dating from the second half of the 16th century should be seen in the context of the master builders and masons who were called to Graz to construct the fortifications. The medieval town was mostly made of wood. According to a report dated 1531, even the Schlossberg castle was "quite old and wooden". When the town wall was refortified in the 16th century, brick construction finally prevailed. The metalwork, timberwork and paintwork were carried out by local craftsmen while the masons and stonemasons were almost exclusively from Italy.

As far as can be ascertained, most of the mason and stonemason families came from the region between Lake Como and Lake Lugano; i.e. from Como (Bertoletti) to Val d'Intelvi (dell'Aglio, Ferrabosco) to Lugano (della Porta de Pone) and its small neighbouring village, Gandria (the Tadei and de Verda families).

These building craftsmen were generally called "maestri comacini" or "Comasken" in the local parlance. This term had been coined during the first big immigration wave in the 16th century. Most of the master builders, masons and stonemasons called in from these regions primarily for the building of fortifications, subsequently settled down in their new homes. This fact is substantiated by the building of a church at Griesplatz (the so-called "Welsche Kirche") and by the establishment of their own guild.

Apart from the outstanding Landhaus facade, many other houses in the historic center still have Renaissance facades that are largely intact. Renaissance houses from the second half of the 16th century typically show corner

IV

Franziskanerkloster, Innenhof
Franciscan Monastery, inner courtyard

ster, Maurer und Steinmetzen in der Folge hier sesshaft und heimisch. Dies dokumentiert sich auch im Bau einer eigenen Kirche, der sog. Welschen Kirche am Griesplatz, und in der Gründung einer eigenen Bruderschaft. Neben der überragenden Landhausfassade besitzen noch viele Häuser in der Altstadt weitgehend intakt erhaltene Renaissancefassaden. Als wesentliches Merkmal des Renaissancebaues in der 2. Hälfte des 16. Jahrhunderts zeigen sich Eckerker, die sich in großer Anzahl erhalten haben, und lombardische Dekorationsformen wie z. B. Grotesken. An Wandflächengestaltungen finden sich auch noch Sgraffiti.

Es ist anzunehmen, dass die hier tätigen Bauleute die Sgraffito-Technik aus ihrer Heimat am Luganer See mitbrachten, wo die von Florenz ausgehenden Kratzputzornamente bereits um 1500 Fuß gefasst hatten. Sgraffiti

oriels, of which there still exist a large number, and Lombardic decorative features, such as grotesques. Wall surfaces are still adorned with sgraffito work.

It is generally assumed that the craftsmen who worked here introduced the sgraffito technique from their native towns by Lake Lugano, where the scratchwork ornaments originating in Florence had already become popular around the year 1500. Sgraffito work can be found on the facade of the Records Wing of the Burg, in the courtyard of the Franciscan Monastery, and in the arcaded courtyards located at Sackstrasse 10 and Hauptplatz 16.

Whereas these facades can be ascribed to the Italian master builders from the region of Lakes Como and Lugano, the narrow facade of no. 10, Hofgasse shows the influence of Roman High Renaissance. It was probably

IV

Sackstraße 10, Renaissancehof
Sackstraße 10, Renaissance courtyard

IV

finden sich an der Fassade des Registraturtraktes der Grazer Burg, im Klosterhof des Franziskanerklosters, in den Arkadenhöfen Sackstraße 10 und Hauptplatz 16.

Während all diese Fassaden, den aus dem Gebiet des Comer und des Luganer Sees kommenden sog. welschen Baumeistern zugeschrieben werden, zeigt die schmale Fassade von Hofgasse Nr. 10 den Einfluss der römischen Hochrenaissance. Sie wird Salustio Peruzzi zugeschrieben, dem Sohn des römischen Baumeisters Baldassare Peruzzi, der ab 1569 als oberster Leiter der Befestigungsanlagen fungierte. Sie ist einzigartig im Grazer Stadtbild und besitzt als Typus einer römischen Hausfassade überregionale Bedeutung im deutschen Sprachraum.

Schlicht und einfach nehmen sich dagegen Erzherzog Karls persönliche Bauten aus. Für den Karlstrakt der Grazer Burg, der als einziges Gliederungselement Renaissance Steinfensterrahmungen aufweist, erstellte der Wiener Hofbaumeister Pietro Ferrabosco aus Laino im Val d'Intelvi den Bauplan.

1596 übernahm Karls ältester Sohn Ferdinand die Regierung und ließ das lutherische Schul- und Kirchenwesen aufheben. Im Jahr 1600 mussten sich die Bürger entscheiden, katholisch zu werden oder auszuwandern.

1619 wurde Erzherzog Ferdinand von Innerösterreich in Frankfurt am Main zum Kaiser gewählt (Ferd. II. 1619–1637) und verlegte seine Residenz nach Wien.

created by Salustio Peruzzi, the son of the Roman master builder Baldassare Peruzzi, who was in charge of the fortifications from 1569. Unparalleled in the townscape of Graz, this typical specimen of a Roman house facade transcends regional boundaries and is of importance for the entire German-speaking world. The buildings constructed by Archduke Charles for his personal use, on the other hand, are notable for their simplicity and unpretentiousness. The plan for the Charles Wing of the Burg, with Renaissance stone window framings as the sole articulating element, was drawn up by the Viennese court architect Pietro Ferraboso from Laino (Val d'Intelvi).

In 1596, Charles' eldest son Ferdinand came to the throne and abolished the Lutheran system of schools and churches. In 1600 the citizens of Graz were made to choose between conversion to the Catholic faith and emigration. In 1619, Archduke Ferdinand of Inner Austria was elected Emperor in Frankfurt on the Main (Ferdinand II, 1619–37), upon which he transferred his residence to Vienna.

Hauptplatz 16, Innenhof, Arkaden mit Sgraffiti (um 1570)

Hauptplatz 16, courtyard arcades with sgraffito work (c. 1570)

Die Baukunst des 17. Jahrhunderts im Übergang von der Renaissance zum Barock

Die Wahl Ferdinands zum Kaiser bedeutete für Graz das Ende als Residenzstadt, jedoch nicht als Hauptstadt Innerösterreichs. Die 1625 neu organisierten Behörden verwalte-

17th-century Architecture between the Renaissance and Baroque

Although Graz ceased to be seat of the court when Ferdinand was elected emperor, it remained the capital of Inner Austria. The authorities, newly organised in 1625, continued

IV

Fassadenansicht mit Schnitt des Straßenübergangs, Plan v. 1832, Bürgergasse 2, (Abb. Kunsttopographie, W. Resch)
View of the facade with section of street crossing, 1832 plan, Bürgergasse 2, (Ill. Art topography, W. Resch)

ten weiterhin die österreichischen Länder.

Nach der Ausweisung der protestantischen Bürger um die Jahrhundertwende verfügte der Kaiser 1628 auch die Ausweisung des protestantischen Adels aus Innerösterreich. Damit war im Wesentlichen die katholische Restauration abgeschlossen.

Zu Beginn des Jahrhunderts entstanden zwei Monumentalbauten – die Jesuitenuniversität und das Mausoleum Ferdinands mit der Katharinenkirche (siehe Stadtkrone).

Wie aus älteren Stichen ersichtlich, wies der Universitätsbau (Bürgergasse 2 a) im Gegensatz zum äußerst schlichten Jesuitenkollegium bereits eine Schauseite mit Fenstergiebeln, Inschrifttafeln und Figurennischen auf (um 1780 bei der Neufassierung abhanden gekommen), die als Manifestation der siegreich durchgeführten Gegenreformation interpretiert werden kann.

to administer the Austrian lands.

Following the expulsion of the Protestant burghers at the turn of the century, the Emperor decreed in 1628 that the Protestant nobility should likewise be expelled from Inner Austria. With this, Catholic restoration was essentially complete.

Two monumental buildings were created at the beginning of the century – the Jesuit University and Ferdinand's Mausoleum with St. Catherine's Church (see "Stadtkrone").

Old engravings show that, unlike the extremely unpretentious Jesuit College, the university building (Bürgergasse 2 a) featured an ornamental wall with gable windows, inscription tablets and niches for statues (lost during refacading works carried out c. 1780), which can be interpreted as a manifestation of the victorious Counter-Reformation.

IV

Franziskanerkirche mit barockem Westturm
Franciscan Church and Baroque western tower

Noch stärker kommt dies beim Mausoleumsbau zum Ausdruck, in dessen Kuppellandschaft Kreuz und Reichsinsignien die enge Verbindung von Kirche und Herrscher demonstrieren. 1614 beauftragte Ferdinand den aus der Lombardei stammenden, in Venedig zum Maler ausgebildeten und seit 1595/96 in Graz tätigen Hofkünstler Giovanni Pietro de Pomis mit dem Bau einer der hl. Katharina geweihten Kirche und einem Mausoleum (siehe Stadtkrone).

Mit dem Baukomplex von Katharinenkirche und dem über ovalem Grundriss errichteten Mausoleum – dem größten Mausoleum der Habsburger – entstand ein imperiales Bauwerk, dessen kunstgeschichtliche Bedeutung in seiner einzigartigen Synthese von schwerer, plastisch durchgearbeiteter Architektur mit einer von Venedig inspirierten, leichten Kuppellandschaft liegt. Im Detail dem Manierismus verhaftet, nimmt die Gesamtanlage bereits barocke Elemente vorweg.

Eine weitere entscheidende Veränderung des Stadtbildes ergab sich auch durch die Errichtung der im Zeichen der Gegenreformation in der 1. Hälfte des 17. Jahrhunderts nach Graz berufenen Klosterniederlassungen. Die Kapuziner und die Karmeliter erhielten große Gebiete in der zu Beginn des 17. Jahrhunderts noch schwächer besiedelten Paulustorvorstadt. Die Augustiner Eremiten dokumentierten sich in der Sporgasse durch langgestreckte Klosterfassaden zu beiden Seiten des Stiegenkirchenaufganges.

An der Murseite wurde die evangelische Stiftsschule, an der auch Johannes Kepler gelehrt hatte, den „Clarissen zu Allerheiligen im Paradeis" übergeben.

Mitte des 17. Jahrhunderts erhielten die Karmelitinnen einen großen Bereich im Kälbernen Viertel.

This effect is enhanced in the mausoleum, in whose dome ensemble the cross and the imperial crown jewels demonstrate the close links between church and monarch. In 1614, Ferdinand commissioned the court artist Giovanni Pietro de Pomis to build a church dedicated to Saint Catherine, as well as a mausoleum (see "Stadtkrone"). The artist came from Lombardy, studied painting in Venice and had been working in Graz since 1595/96.

The building complex of St. Catherine's Church and the mausoleum erected on an oval base – the largest Habsburg mausoleum – represents an imperial building whose importance for art history lies in its unique synthesis of heavy three-dimensional architecture topped by a light and airy landscape of Venetian-style domes. While the details are rooted in Mannerism, the structure as a whole anticipates Baroque elements.

The townscape underwent a further substantial change when new monasteries, having been invited to Graz to assist the Counter-Reformation, were established in the first half of the 17th century. Capuchins and Carmelites both received large tracts of land in the Paulus Gate quarter, which was still rather sparsely settled at the beginning of the 17th century. The Augustinian hermits settled in Sporgasse behind long stretched-out monastery facades on either side of the stairs leading to Stiegenkirche. On the side bordering the river Mur, the Protestant foundation school where Johannes Kepler had taught was turned over to the order of St. Clare who founded the "Clarissen zu Allerheiligen im Paradeis". In the middle of the 17th century the Carmelite nuns received a large area in the quarter known as the "Kälbernes Viertel". In addition to these large monastic settlements, the Franciscans started a tower in

IV

Palais Kollonitsch, Schmiedgasse
Palais Kollonitsch, Schmiedgasse

Neben diesen weitläufigen Klosteranlagen verstärkte auch der ab 1636 erbaute Turm der Franziskanerkirche die kirchliche Präsenz im zuvor fast ausschließlich von bürgerlichen Profanbauten geprägten Stadtgebiet.

Obwohl Graz seine Funktion als Residenzstadt verloren hatte, entstanden im 2. Viertel des 17. Jahrhunderts eine Reihe von Adelspalais. Als Bauherr fungierte vor allem der im Zuge der Gegenreformation und Güterkonfiskation groß gewordene katholische Adel. Zu nennen wäre hier vor allem das Palais der Eggenberger in der Sackstraße 16 (heutige Neue Galerie) oder die mächtige Vierflügel-Anlage des Palais Kollonitsch (Schmiedgasse 21) mit Arkaden-Innenhof. Das Straßenbild der Schmiedgasse wird im unteren Drittel wesentlich von der Spätrenaissance-Fassade mit ihren auf Säulen ruhenden polygonalen Eckerkern bestimmt.

1636 which further emphasised the ecclesiastical presence in a municipal area hitherto characterised almost exclusively by secular structures.

Although Graz had lost its function as the seat of the court, several noble families built their palaces in the town in the second quarter of the 17th century, among them prominent Catholic noblemen who had aggrandised themselves in the wake of the Counter-Reformation and resultant confiscation of property. Foremost among these are the palais of the Eggenbergs at Sackstrasse 16 (today's New Gallery) and the mighty four-winged building of Palais Kollonitsch (Schmiedgasse 21) with an arcaded inner courtyard. The lower third of Schmiedgasse is dominated by its late Renaissance facade with cant-bay corner oriels resting on columns.

IV

Landeszeughaus, Eingangsportal
mit den Skulpturen Mars und Minerva, 1643/44

Armoury,
with sculptures of Mars and Minerva, 1643/44

Einen der bauhistorisch bedeutendsten Bauten dieser Zeitspanne stellt das ab 1642 von Santino Solari erbaute landschaftliche Zeughaus dar, das schon durch seine Funktion als Waffenkammer eine solitäre Stellung einnimmt.

Den schlichten Zweckbau akzentuiert das monumentale Spätrenaissance-Portal von Giovanni Mamolo, die seitlichen Nischenfiguren Mars und Minerva stellen die qualitätsvollste Grazer Bauplastik dar und sind stilistisch bereits dem Frühbarock zuzuordnen.

One of the most outstanding buildings of this period is the Styrian armoury built by Santino Solari from 1642 onwards. It derives its unique position primarily from its role as an arsenal. The plain functional structure is accentuated by the monumental late Renaissance portal of Giovanni Mamolo. The statues in the niches at its sides, Mars and Minerva, can be ranked as the best architectural sculptures in Graz. Stylistically, they anticipate early Baroque.

IV

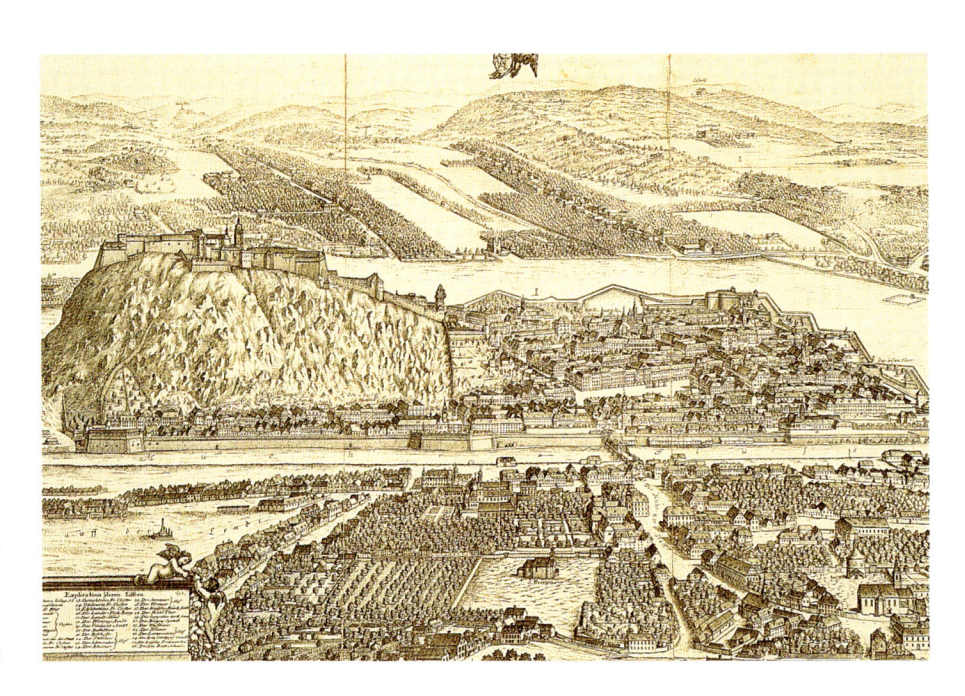

Stadtansicht, Graz gegen Osten,
Andreas Trost, Kupferstich, 1695

Eastern view of Graz,
Andreas Trost, engraving, 1695

Barock – Die Zeit unter Kaiser Leopold I. bis Maria Theresia

1660, drei Jahre nach seinem Regierungsantritt, nahm Kaiser Leopold I. die prunkvolle Erbhuldigung in Graz entgegen. Auch sein Entschluss, seine Hochzeit mit Claudia Felicitas von Tirol in Graz abzuhalten, gab erneut Anlass zu umfangreichen Feiern. Die Feiern fanden im schönsten Barockschloss der Steiermark, im Schloss Eggenberg, statt. Dieses befindet sich im westlichen Teil der Stadt. Ein negativer Anlass dagegen war die türkische Kriegserklärung von 1663, wonach die Befestigungsanlage wieder instand gesetzt und alle außerhalb der Stadt gelegenen Häuser abgebrochen werden mussten. Zur Türkengefahr kam in den folgenden Jahren die Pest, die ungefähr ein Fünftel der Bevölkerung hinwegraffte (um 1680 dürfte die Ein-

The Baroque Period from Emperor Leopold I to Maria Theresa

In 1660, three years after his accession to the throne, the magnificent ceremony of the oath of allegiance to Emperor Leopold I took place in Graz. His decision to hold his wedding with Claudia Felicitas of Tyrol in Graz gave rise to further sumptuous celebrations. The festivities were held at Schloss Eggenberg, Styria's most beautiful Baroque palace, located in the western part of Graz.
Activities of a different kind became necessary when in 1663 the Turks declared war on Austria. The fortifications had to be repaired, and all buildings outside the town were demolished. The Turkish peril was further aggravated when the Black Death struck, killing about one fifth of the population (the inhabitants of Graz numbered approximately

IV

Raubergasse 10, „Altes Joanneum", ehem. St. Lambrechter Stiftshof

Raubergasse 10, "Altes Joanneum", court of former St. Lambrecht Abbey

wohnerzahl von Graz ca. 15.000 betragen haben). Nach dem Sieg über die Türken 1683 wurden von der Grazer Bevölkerung Pestsäulen errichtet, die noch heute ganz wesentliche Akzente im urbanen Platzbereich darstellen, wie z. B. die barocke Mariensäule am Platz vor dem Eisernen Tor.

1705 verstarb Kaiser Leopold. 1728 war ein weiteres wichtiges Jahr für die Grazer Stadtgeschichte. Da die innerösterreichischen Stände 1720 die weibliche Erbfolge (Pragmatische Sanktion) anerkannt hatten, kam Kaiser Karl VI. nach Graz, um sich der Zeremonie der Erbhuldigungsfeiern zu unterziehen.

Die Erbhuldigungsfeier von 1728 gab den Anlass für die großzügige Neupflasterung und die Einführung einer Straßenbeleuchtung. Vier Tage vor der Ankunft des Kaisers erstrahlten die Grazer Gassen zum ersten Mal im Schein der Laternen. Auf Kosten der Landstände wurde die Feier, die die letzte steirische Erbhuldigung sein sollte, in einem Kupferstichwerk festgehalten.

Das von Deyerlsberg 1740 herausgegebene Erbhuldigungswerk stellt mit seinen detaillierten Stadtansichten eine der wichtigsten Quellen für die Baugeschichte der Stadt Graz dar. Die bekanntesten Stadtveduten daraus sind die Kupferstiche von Andreas Trost, der 1699 die Stadt gegen Osten und Westen fast topographisch genau wierdergegeben hatte. Während in Wien unter Leopold I. schon zu Beginn der sechziger Jahre der gegliederte Palastbau einsetzte, entstand in Graz erst mit dem Bau des St. Lambrechter Hofes in der Raubergasse 1665/74 die erste barocke Fassadengliederung mit geschoßweiser Pilastergliederung. Den Hauptakzent bildet die Hermen-Pilasterreihe des zweiten Obergeschoßes mit dem plastisch gestalteten Kranzgesims. Der St. Lambrechter Hof ist ein Alterswerk des aus Roveredo im Misoxer-

15,000 in 1680). After the Turks had been defeated in 1683, the surviving people of Graz erected plague columns, which are still very essential features of the squares, such as the Baroque Our Lady's Column on the square in front of the Iron Gate.

Emperor Leopold died in 1705. 1728 was another important year in the history of Graz. After the Inner Austrian estates had recognised the succession of women (Pragmatic Sanction) in 1720, Emperor Charles VI came to Graz for the festivities arranged for the ceremony of the oath of allegiance.

The town used the occasion of the celebrations of 1728 to have the streets newly paved and street lighting installed. Four days before the Emperor's arrival, the streets of Graz were illuminated for the first time by lanterns. This celebration, which was to be the last of its kind held in Styria, was captured in a collection of copperplate engravings paid for by the Styrian estates. This work, published by Deyerlsberg in 1740, features detailed views of the town, which makes it one of the most important sources for architectural history in Graz. Its best-known town vedute are the copper engravings by Andreas Trost, who depicted the town in 1699 from the east and west with an almost perfect topographic accuracy.

While the fashion for articulated palace architecture had began in Vienna under Leopold I in the 1660s, Graz received its first Baroque facade arrangement with floor-by-floor pilasters only when St. Lambrecht's Court was built in Raubergasse (1665–74). Its major feature is the row of pilasters representing herms on the second upper storey with the moulded cornice. St. Lambrecht's Court is a late work of Domenico Sciassio (1599/1603–1679) from Roveredo in the Vale Mesolcina (the Grisons). It is strongly influ-

IV

Hauptplatz 9–11 mit Luegghaus
Hauptplatz 9-11 with "Luegg-Haus"

tal (Graubünden) stammenden Domenico Sciassio (1599/1603–1679). Sciassio, der mit Abt Pierin von St. Lambrecht 1652 eine Romreise unternommen hatte, zeigte sich beim Lambrechter Hof vor allem in der grotesken Bauplastik des Kranzgesimses dem comaskisch-lombardischen Renaissance-Formengut verhaftet.

Eine andere charakteristische Gestaltungsform zeigt sich in den Stuckfassaden, deren Schweifwerk (Hauptplatz 16) oder Akanthusranken mit Fruchtgehängen (Hauptplatz 9, Luegghaus) die Wandfläche rein ornamental überziehen. Eine interessante Mischform von Putzbändergliederung mit vegetabilen Stuckformen weist die Fassade des zweiten Luegg-Hauses, Hauptplatz 11, auf. Bei diesen Häusern erfolgte kein Neubau, sondern nur ein Umbau mit Neufassadierung, wobei man Teile des Altbestandes, wie die spätgoti-

enced by the forms and designs of the Renaissance style of the Como and Lombardy region which Sciassio had absorbed from various theoretical works on architecture and on a journey to Rome made with Abbot Pierin of St. Lambrecht in 1652 and which are particularly evident in the grotesquely sculptured cornice of St. Lambrecht's Court.

Another typical feature is the stucco facades with their scrolls (Hauptplatz 16) and acanthus tendrils with fruit festoons (Hauptplatz 9, Luegg-Haus), which cover the wall surfaces for purely ornamental purposes. The facade of the second Luegg-Haus (Hauptplatz 11) shows an interesting mixture of plaster bands with vegetable stucco forms. These houses were not rebuilt but converted and given new facades, while parts of the old buildings, such as the late-Gothic ground-floor arcades of the Luegg Houses, were retained and inte-

IV

Mehlplatz mit Blick gegen die Prokopigasse
Mehlplatz, view toward Prokopigasse

schen Erdgeschoßlauben der Luegghäuser integrierte. Diese an Südtiroler und oberitalienische Laubenganghäuser erinnernde Architektur stellt einen der interessantesten architektonischen Blickpunkte am Hauptplatz dar.

Parallel zu den im 4. Viertel des 17. Jahrhunderts stärker einsetzenden frühbarocken Fassadengliederungen zeichnet sich in den Innenräumen der Profanbauten eine zunehmende Vorliebe für Stuckdecken ab, wobei eine ähnliche Entwicklung wie an den Fassaden zu verfolgen ist. Einerseits bilden flache Putzbänder streng geometrische Gliederungsformen, anderseits werden naturalistische Putti, Fruchtgehänge mit Knorpel- oder Schweifwerk zu stark plastischen Rahmungen um Mittelspiegel oder Kartuschen verdichtet (Mehlplatz 1).

Wie die Baumeister des 16. Jahrhunderts fast ausschließlich aus dem Gebiet zwischen Comer und Luganer See stammen, so kommen die Stuckateure des 17. Jahrhunderts aus dem Misoxertal (Graubünden).

Der Höhepunkt der italienisch orientierten frühbarocken Deckenstuckierung liegt im letzten Drittel des 17. Jahrhunderts (Decken im Stiegenhaus des Palais Stubenberg (Hans-Sachs-Gasse 7), Palais Kollonitsch (Schmiedgasse 21), Palais Dietrichstein (Burggasse 9).

Zunehmende Bedeutung erhielten auch die Treppenanlagen, die durchwegs Steinbalustraden mit einer charakteristischen kantigen Balusterform aufweisen (Karmeliterplatz 6 oder Hans-Sachs-Gasse 1).

Als die Herberstein um 1690 ihr Stadtpalais errichteten, wurden vier Häuser unter Beibehaltung eines Renaissance-Erkers und des Einfahrtstores zusammengefügt. Die geringe Aufmerksamkeit, die man der Fassade beimaß, steht im größten Widerspruch zur zwei-

grated in the conversion. This architecture is evocative of South Tyrolean and Upper Italian galleried houses and represents one of the most interesting architectural elements on the Hauptplatz.

Parallel to the early Baroque facade designs increasingly used in the last quarter of the 17th century, secular architecture showed a growing preference for stucco ceilings, which developed along the same lines as the facades: flat plaster bands forming strictly geometric patterns were juxtaposed with naturalistic putti, fruit festoons with scrolls and spirals to form heavily moulded frames for central mirrors or cartouches (Mehlplatz 1)

Just as the master builders of the 16th century came almost exclusively from the region between Lakes Como and Lugano, the stuccoists of the 17th century were from the Vale Mesolcina (Grisons).

Italianate early Baroque ceiling stuccowork reaches its peak in the last third of the 17th century, with the ceilings of the stairwell of Palais Stubenberg (Hans Sachsgasse 7), Palais Kollonitsch (Schmiedgasse 21) and Palais Dietrichstein (Burggasse 9).

Much decorative care was also devoted to the staircases, most of which had stone balustrades with banisters of a characteristically angular form (houses on Karmeliterplatz and in Hans Sachsgasse 1).

When the Herberstein family built their town palais in c. 1690, four houses were joined together, retaining a Renaissance oriel and the entrance gate. Little attention was paid to the facade, but much was lavished on the double-flight staircase in the courtyard: due to its loggia conception it constitutes one of the most noteworthy Styrian staircases of the late 17th century and suggests Italian models, presumably from Genoa or Venice.

Hans-Sachs-Gasse 7, ehem. Palais Stubenberg, später Palais Welsersheimb

Hans-Sachs-Gasse 7, former Palais Stubenberg which became Palais Welsersheimb

seitig stehenden Treppenanlage im Hof; mit ihrer Loggienkonzeption stellt sie eine der bedeutendsten steirischen Treppenanlagen des ausgehenden 17. Jahrhunderts dar und läßt auf italienische Vorbilder – vermutlich in Genua oder Venedig – schließen.

Unmittelbar nach der Jahrhundertwende entstanden die beiden bedeutendsten barocken Stadtpalais. 1702/03 das Palais Wildenstein (Paulustorgasse 8) und 1702/05 das Palais Attems (Sackstraße 17).

Das Palais Wildenstein besitzt über dem als Sockel konzipierten Erdgeschoß eine in Österreich einzigartige kolossale Säulengliederung mit 22 elliptischen, in Pilasternischen versenkten Säulen, die als Schauwand einem älteren Bau vorgelegt wurden.

Dem gegenüber weist das anstelle von sechs älteren Häusern errichtete Palais Attems auch eine barocke Raumstruktur und die ein-

The two most important town palais of the Baroque period were built shortly after the turn of the century: Palais Wildenstein (1702–03, Paulustorgasse 8) and Palais Attems (1702–05, Sackstrasse 17). The former is a design unique in Austria: colossal columns articulate the facade, rising from the ground floor socle in 22 elliptical columns sunk in the pilaster recesses of a curtain wall that hides the original wall.

Palais Attems, built in place of six older houses, also features a Baroque room arrangement, as well as the only wall and ceiling furnishings in the town that have been preserved largely intact. The facades of the U-shaped main body of the building are instrumented above the two-storey socle zone by a small pilaster arrangement with richly detailed window framings, while the entrance axis is accentuated by a monumen-

IV

Palais Attems
Palais Attems

zige im Stadtgebiet weitgehend erhaltene barocke Wand- und Deckenausstattung auf. Die Fassaden des u-förmigen Baukörpers sind über der zweigeschossigen Sockelzone durch eine kleine Pilasterordnung mit reich gegliederten Fensterrahmungen instrumentiert, die Eingangsachse wird durch die monumentale über drei Achsen reichende und mit einem Balkon bekrönte Portal-Anlage hervorgehoben. Die beiden Palais sind in ihren Gestaltungsprinzipien weder miteinander vergleichbar noch aus der heimischen Tradition erklärbar. Für das Gesamtkonzept dürften die gräflichen Bauherren verantwortlich zeichnen, wobei sie sich unter dem Einfluss architekturtheoretischer Werke wohl an international renommierten Bauten orientierten, jedoch zu eigenständigen Leistungen fanden, die unter dem Begriff „Kavaliersarchitektur" zu reihen sind.

tal portal ensemble that extends over three axes and is crowned by a balcony.
The two palais are entirely at variance in their architectural principles, and cannot be traced to local tradition. Their general design concept appear to have originated from the ducal clients themselves who, influenced by works on architectural theory, drew on ideas from internationally renowned buildings, but achieved solutions in their own right that are known as "Kavaliersarchitektur", architecture by noble dilettanti.
Structures to be judged on their own merits are the Baroque portals added on to older buildings, such as the atlas-flanked portal of Hans Sachsgasse 1 and the projecting portal of Palais Khuenburg (Sackstrasse 18), whose balustrade supported by columns and slanting wall pillars makes it one of the highest-quality portals of the high Baroque.

Palais Attems, Innenhof, Fassadendetail
Palais Attems, inner courtyard, detail of facade

Als solitäre Bauformen können auch die nachträglich eingebauten Barockportale gewertet werden, das Atlantenportal von Hans-Sachs-Gasse 1 und der Portalvorbau des Palais Khuenburg (Sackstraße 18), der mit seiner von Säulen und schräggestellten Wandpfeilern getragenen Balustrade eines der qualitätsvollsten Portale des Hochbarock darstellt.

Zu Beginn des 18. Jahrhunderts ist ein stilistischer Bruch in der Stuckdekoration feststellbar, der sich sowohl in der Innenausstattung als auch an den Fassaden der Bürgerhäuser abzeichnet.

Besonders deutlich wird der Umbruch an dem bereits besprochenen Palais Attems; während sich die Fassadenstuckatur mit plastischen Vasen, Festons und Grotesken noch dem italienischen Formengut verpflichtet zeigt, werden die Stuckdecken im Inneren bereits überwiegend von ornamentalem, an die Fläche gebundenem Laubwerk geprägt. Als schönstes und vermutlich spätestes Beispiel einer barocken Stuckfassade mit Nischenmadonna dürfte das Bürgerhaus, Kapaunplatz 2 zu bezeichnen sein, dessen reich gegliedertes Laub-, Bandl- und Gitterwerk bereits Rokokoansätze erkennen läßt.

The change in stucco styles at the beginning of the 18th century is clearly noticeable on interior walls as well as on the facades of the burgher houses. This break manifests itself in particular in the Palais Attems: while the facade stucco work with its plastic vases, festoons and grimacing heads still shows the influence of Italian forms, the stucco ceilings inside are already characterised to a large extent by a purely ornamental foliage which is bound to the surface. The most beautiful and probably latest example of a Baroque stucco facade with a recessed Madonna is the burgher house at Kapaunplatz 2, whose richly structured foliage, strapwork and latticework already show the first signs of the new Rococo style.

Die bedeutendsten Bauwerke der Grazer Altstadt

Die Stadtkrone

Burg, Domkirche, Mausoleum, Alte Universität und Priesterseminar bilden die sogenannte Stadtkrone, ein in Jahrhunderten gewachsenes, einzigartiges, architektonisches und kunsthistorisches Ensemble; wobei vor allem die Kuppellandschaft des Mausoleumkomplexes die Krone eines Stadtbildes assoziiert.

The Main Buildings of the Historic Center

"Stadtkrone"

The so-called Stadtkrone ("Crown of the Town") is a cluster of major buildings: Burg, Cathedral, Mausoleum, Old University and Seminary, a unique ensemble of great importance in terms of architecture and art, evolved over centuries of urban development. It takes its name and resemblance to a

IV

Stadtkrone, Luftaufnahme mit Burg, Dom, Mausoleum und Priesterseminar

Stadtkrone, aerial photograph of the Cathedral, Mausoleum and Seminary

Diese erhebt sich markant über der vielfältigen Dachlandschaft des historischen Stadtzentrums. Sie begrenzt den gewachsenen Stadtkern zum Stadtpark hin und ist ein Kontrapunkt zum geschäftigen Treiben um den Hauptplatz und den Schlossberg. Die Grazer Stadtkrone ist aber mehr als ein bauliches Ensemble. In keiner anderen österreichischen Landeshauptstadt hat sich das weltliche und geistige Zentrum des Landes so eng miteinander verbunden und außerhalb der bürgerlichen Marktsiedlung manifestiert.

So ist heute die Grazer Burg der Sitz der Steirischen Landesregierung und die Alte Universität die Wiege der modernen Karl-Franzens-Universität, die 1995 ihre 100-Jahrfeier begehen konnte.

crown mainly from the domes that rise from the Mausoleum and soar above the variegated roofscape of the historical town center. The assembly delimits the extended core of the historic center in the City Park direction and provides a deft counterpoint to the bustle of the streets around the main square and Schlossberg. But the Stadtkrone is more than just an architectural ensemble. In no other provincial capital of Austria has there been such a close association between spiritual and temporal centres, manifesting itself outside and distinct from the burghers' settlement.

Today, the Burg is the residence of the Styrian provincial government, and the Old University is the cradle of its modern successor, Karl-Franzens University, which celebrated its 100th anniversary in 1995.

IV

Geschichtliche und bauliche Entwicklung

Geschichtlich fassbar wird der Bereich der Stadtkrone im 12. Jahrhundert, als der Grundherr des Grazer Bodens, der Hochfreie Bernhard von Stübing, bald nach 1122 die bisher unbesiedelte Aulandschaft entlang des linken Murufers mit Dörfern besetzte und sich eine neue Herrschaftsburg auf dem Schlossberg errichten ließ.

Zur gleichen Zeit entstand der herrschaftliche Meierhof als Vorläufer der Stadtburg, die Eigenkirche St. Ägydius und ein erster Straßenmarkt zwischen Schlossberg und Mur. Wie in vielen mittelalterlichen steirischen Städten lag die Pfarrkirche von Graz somit außerhalb der Marktsiedlung. Die alte Ägydiuskirche dürfte bedeutend kleiner als die heutige gotische Domkirche gewesen sein. Umgeben von einem Friedhof mit abschließender Wehrmauer wird man sich die alte romanische Pfarrkirche in der Art eines Kirchenkastells, auf das Marktleben des Städtchen zu seinen Füßen herabblickend, vorstellen können.

Die wichtigsten Taten für Graz setzte Kaiser Friedrich III. durch den Bau einer neuen Residenz – einer Stadtburg in der NO-Ecke der mittelalterlichen Stadtmauer – und durch den Neubau der alten Pfarrkirche St. Ägydius (heutige Domkirche), die er mit einem Gang über der Hofgasse verbinden ließ.

Es folgte die Doppelwendeltreppe Kaiser Maximilians, ein weltweit berühmtes Juwel spätgotischer Baukunst.

Vom Karlstrakt der Grazer Burg aus wurde der souveräne Staat Innerösterreich verwaltet. Weitere Bauten in unmittelbarer Nähe folgten, wie das Priesterseminar, die Alte Universität der Jesuiten und das Mausoleum Kaiser Ferdinands II.

Den Schwerpunkt bilden die Bauten der Jesuiten, die 200 Jahre lang diesen Bereich

Historical and Structural Development

We find the first records of the Stadtkrone in the 12th century, when Bernhard von Stübing, allodiary and demesne lord of the land on which Graz was to develop, had villages built into the natural forests along the left river bank soon after 1122 and ordered a manor seat for himself on the Schlossberg.

At about the same time, the manorial farm was established on the site where later the Burg was to be built, together with the proprietory church of St. Ägydius and the first street market between Schlossberg and the river Mur. As in many other Styrian medieval towns, the parish church was located outside the market settlement. The original church of St. Ägydius appears to have been very much smaller than today's Gothic cathedral church. Encircled by a cemetery and fortifying wall, the Romanesque parish church should be viewed as a cross between a church and a castle looking down on the busy market life in the little town at its feet.

A milestone in the development of Graz was reached by Emperor Frederick III when he built his new residence in the north-eastern corner of the medieval town wall and rebuilt the old parish church (today's cathedral), linking the two by a corridor across Hofgasse.

Emperor Maximilian followed with the double-spiral staircase, a gem of late Gothic architecture famous world-wide.

The sovereign state of Inner Austria was governed from the Charles Wing of the Burg. Other buildings soon gathered nearby, among them the Seminary, the Old University of the Jesuits and the Mausoleum of Emperor Ferdinand II. Jesuits contributed most to the construction activities, putting their mark on the area for two centuries: their buildings still make up a major part of the ensemble.

IV

wesentlich prägten und deren Bautätigkeit immer noch einen bedeutenden Anteil am Ensemble der Stadtkrone hat.

Die Stadtkrone wird baulich in erster Linie von friederizianischer Gotik und welscher Renaissance geprägt. Das Mausoleum mit der Katharinenkirche stellt den architektonisch interessantesten Baukomplex dar. Erweisen sich die Gesamtanlage und die markante Fassade als einzigartige Dokumente einer Baugesinnung an der Wende von der Renaissance zum Barock, so ist es vor allem die weit sichtbare Kuppellandschaft, die dem Stadtbild die charakteristische Silhouette verleiht. Die Größe und Bedeutung der Barockzeit liegt vor allem in der Innenausstattung von Dom und Katharinenkirche (Mausoleum).

Erst beim Gesamtumbau des Jesuitenkonviktes, des heutigen Domherrenhofes, entstand der einzige auch nach außen wirkende Barockbau der Stadtkrone.

Die Baumeister der Stadtkrone

Über die Baumeister der gotischen Periode unter Friedrich III. bestehen kaum Nachrichten. Für den Bau des Domes wird der Schwabe Hans Niesenberger vermutet, der 1459 beim Regensburger Hüttentag als Meister von Graz auftrat.

Bei jüngst durchgeführten bauarchäologischen Untersuchungen konnten in der Friedrichskapelle der Burg fünf Steinmetzzeichen aus der frühesten Erbauungszeit freigelegt werden.

Besser dagegen sind die Bauten der Renaissance dokumentiert, die noch heute im Wesentlichen die Stadtkrone prägen. Als Baumeister ist sicher der vom Kaiser als oberster Bauleiter für den Neubau der Befestigungsanlagen nach Graz berufene Domenico dell' Aglio anzunehmen, dessen Ruhm noch durch

In its building styles, the Stadtkrone is dominated by the Gothic of Frederick and the Italian Renaissance. The Mausoleum and St. Catherine's Church are the most interesting complex in architectural terms. While the structure as a whole and its striking facade are unique expressions of building design at the threshold of Renaissance and Baroque, it is the domescape, visible from afar, that lends the city its characteristic silhouette. The might and power of the Baroque period is displayed mainly in the interiors of the cathedral and St. Catherine's (Mausoleum). In fact, the only building of the Stadtkrone visibly Baroque from outside appearance is the Domherrenhof, the former Jesuit convent which was converted for use of the canons of the cathedral.

The Builders of the Stadtkrone

Little is known of the builders of the Gothic period presided over by Frederick III. The cathedral appears to have been built by Hans Niesenberger from Swabia, who presented himself as the Master of Graz at the Regensburg assembly of stonemasons' lodges in 1459. Recent archaeological investigations excavated five stonemasons' marks from the earliest construction period in the Frederick Chapel of the Burg.

More information is available from the Renaissance buildings which are still the most numerous of the Stadtkrone ensemble. They were almost certainly built by Domenico dell'Aglio, who was called in by the Emperor to serve as the senior supervisor when the fortifications were built, and whose fame is further enhanced by the Landhaus.

das Grazer Landhaus wachgehalten wird.

Für den Bau des Karlstraktes ließ Erzherzog Karl Pläne vom Wiener Hofbaumeister Pietro Ferrabosco erstellen. Den weiteren Burgzubau, den sog. Registraturtrakt, leitete dessen Bruder M. Antonio Tadei.

Für den Bau des Jesuitenkollegiums konnte Vinzenz de Verda als verantwortlicher Baumeister erforscht werden.

Diese Baumeister wie auch die namentlich bekannten Maurer und Steinmetzen kamen ab der 2. Hälfte des 16. Jahrhunderts für den Neubau des Befestigungsgürtels nach Graz (siehe Altstadt). Sie stammten fast ausnahmslos aus dem Gebiet zwischen Comer und Luganer See. Ein Gebiet, das seit Anfang des 16. Jahrhunderts auf Italien und Schweiz verteilt, ursprünglich geschlossen zum Einflussbereich und zur Diözese Comos gehörte. Meist kamen mehrere Mitglieder einer Familie nach Graz, zum Teil kehrten sie nach Jahren wieder in ihre Heimat zurück oder wurden in Graz heimisch. Entscheidend ist, dass diese „Welschen", wie sie allgemein hießen, bzw. „Comasken", wie sie in der Architekturgeschichte bezeichnet werden, nicht nur am Festungsbau tätig waren, sondern auch für die großzügige Erneuerung der Stadtgebäude in der Zeit als Residenzstadt Innerösterreichs herangezogen wurden (siehe Altstadt).

For his own wing in the Burg, Archduke Charles commissioned designs from Pietro Ferrabosco, court builder in Vienna. His brother, M. Antonio Tadei, supervised the construction of another annex, the Records Wing.

The Jesuit college is generally attributed to Vinzenz de Verda.

These master builders, together with the masons and stonemasons whose names have been handed down to us, arrived in Graz in the second half of the 16th century when the fortifications were built. Virtually all of them came from the region between Lake Como and Lake Lugano, which originally belonged to the diocese of Como before it was divided between Italy and Switzerland in the early 16th century. Usually several members of a family worked in Graz, and some of them returned after many years or even settled down in Graz. Known locally as the "Welschen" (Italians) and in architectural history as the "maestri comacini", they were employed not just to build the fortifications but also to carry out extensive reconstruction work on the town buildings when Graz was the seat of the Dukes of Inner Austria (see historic center).

IV

Burgeingang, Hofgasse 15
Entrance to the Burg Hofgasse 15

Die Burg-Anlage

Von der ursprünglichen Stadtburg Kaiser Friedrichs III. sind noch eine gotische Halle, das spätgotische Kapellenzimmer und die einzigartige gotische Doppelwendeltreppe, die Kaiser Maximilian, Sohn Friedrichs III., um 1499 errichten ließ, erhalten.

Die gotische Doppelwendeltreppe

Der polygonale Treppenhausturm von 1499 am Durchgang zum zweiten Burghof ist der einzig erhaltene Teil des unter Kaiser Maximilian erbauten Burgflügels, der die unter seinem Vater entstandenen Burgbauten miteinander verband (im oberen Drittel befinden sich römische Grabsteine, die Maximilian 1506 hier einmauern ließ).
Durch ein spätgotisches Tor aus Rotmarmor

Burg

Of the castle originally inhabited by Emperor Frederick III, the Gothic hall, a late Gothic chapel and the unique Gothic double-spiral staircase built by his son, Emperor Maximilian in c. 1499, have survived.

The Gothic Double-Spiral Staircase

The polygonal stairwell of 1499, sitting across the passage to the second castle court, is the only remaining part of a wing built by Maximilian to connect the castle buildings erected during under his father's rule (its upper third is decorated with the Roman tombstones Maximilian had placed there in 1506).
A late Gothic doorway of red marble offers

IV

Doppelwendeltreppe, Grazer Burg, 1499
Double-spiral staircase, Burg, 1499

gelangt man zur viergeschossigen Doppelwendeltreppe, die sich in steilen Windungen nach oben dreht. Die jeweils gegenläufigen Stiegen vereinigen sich immer wieder in den gemeinsamen Zwischenpodesten. Mit ihrer Doppelläufigkeit sowie der großteils freitragenden Steinkonstruktion gehört die Doppelwendeltreppe der Grazer Burg zu den bedeutendsten spätgotischen Treppenanlagen Europas und stellt ein Meisterwork der Steinmetzkunst einer zu Ende gehenden Epoche dar.

Der unter Erzherzog Karl 1570/71 errichtete „Karlsbau" ist als Burgtrakt weitgehend erhalten und bildet heute als Sitz des Landeshauptmannes mit seinen Festsälen den ideelen Kern der Burganlage. Errichtet wurde der Trakt zwischen dem rückwärtigen Friedrichsbau in der NO-Ecke der mittelalterlichen Stadtmauer und dem östlichen Stadttor,

access to the four-storied double-spiral staircase which winds upwards in steep turns. The two flights of the staircase, running in opposite directions, join at shared landings. With its dog-legged design and mostly self-supported stone structure, the double-spiral staircase at the Graz Burg ranks among the major late Gothic staircases in Europe as a masterpiece of stonemasonry marking the end of an era.

The "Karlsbau" or Charles Wing, which Archduke Charles built in 1570–71, has remained largely intact. Used today as the Styrian governor's residence, its rooms and in particular its ceremonial halls constitute the spiritual core of the Burg. The wing was fitted in between Frederick's building at the northeastern corner of the medieval town wall and the eastern town gate, the "Burgtor". This Gothic gate, constructed in 1336–39, with its

IV

dem sog. Burgtor. Dieser 1336/1339 errichtete gotische Torbau mit beidseitigen spitzen Steintorrahmen ist das älteste noch erhaltene Stadttor von Graz.

Dagegen besticht das monumentale Renaissance-Portal (1554 von Domenico dell'Aglio), in den ersten Burghof führend, durch seine schlichte Monumentalität und präzise Steinquaderung. In dieser Konzeption entspricht es vollkommen den Portalentwürfen Sebastiano Serlios, dessen architekturtheoretisches Werk die vermutlich verbreitetste Arbeitsunterlage für die in Europa tätigen „welschen" Baumeister bildete.

Der Registraturtrakt

Der langgestreckte Registraturtrakt wurde ebenfalls unter Erzherzog Karl II. 1581/85 vom welschen Baumeister M. Antonio Tadei errichtet. Von kunsthistorischer Bedeutung erweisen sich die Sgraffiti – ornamentale Kratzputzverzierungen an der Fassade. Tadei, ebenso aus dem Kreis der welschen Baumeister stammend, brachte die Sgraffito-Technik von seiner Heimat am Luganer See mit, wo die von Florenz ausgehenden Kratzputzornamente bereits um 1500 Fuß gefasst hatten.

Das Priesterseminar
(ehemals Jesuitenkollegium)

1572 berief der katholische Landesfürst Erzherzog Karl II. von Innerösterreich die Jesuiten von Ingolstadt (Deutschland) nach Graz, um von hier aus wirkungsvoll gegen den immer stärker werdenden Protestantismus vorgehen zu können.

Der gewaltige Baukomplex wurde von dem aus Gandria bei Lugano stammenden und beim Festungsbau tätigen Baumeister Vin-

pointed stone frames on either side, is the oldest surviving town gate of Graz.

It stands in contrast with the monumental Renaissance portal (Domenico dell'Aglio, 1554), which grants access to the first castle court and which is notable for its plain, unadorned grandiosity and the precision of its parallelepipedal stones. Its design mirrors the portals drawn by Sebastiano Serlio whose oeuvre on architectural theory had a profound influence on the Italian master builders working all over Europe.

The Records Wing

The "Registraturtrakt", a long drawn-out wing housing government records, was built by Marc Antonio Tadei, also of Italy, under Archduke Charles II, in 1581–85. An interesting feature from an art history perspective is the ornamental sgraffito scratchwork decorating the facade. Tadei, another member of the group of Italian architects, brought the sgraffito technique from his home on Lake Lugano, where the fashion, originating in Florence, had already taken hold by 1500.

The Seminary
(former Jesuit college)

In 1572, Archduke Charles II, the Catholic prince of Inner Austria, invited the Jesuits of Ingolstadt (Germany) to Graz in order to mount an effective attack against the growing Protestant movement.

Construction on their vast complex began in 1572. It was built by Vinzenz de Verda, who came from Gandria near Lugano and who also worked on the fortifications. The theolo-

IV

Priesterseminar, ehem. Jesuitenkollegium, Arkadenhof

Seminary, former Jesuit college, arcaded courtyard

zenz de Verda ab 1572 errichtet.
Das Grazer Kollegium gehört zu den ersten deutschen Jesuitenkollegien, neben Augsburg, München und Koblenz, und es zählt auch zu den größten in diesem Jahrhundert. Während ein Großteil der Kollegien des 16. Jahrhunderts in den folgenden Jahrhunderten umgebaut und barockisiert wurden, entspricht das Grazer Kollegium als einziges noch weitgehend den ursprünglichen Bauprinzipien und ist daher ein für die gesamte deutsche Ordensprovinz bedeutendes Dokument der frühen Jesuitenarchitektur. Der eigentlichen Größe diese Bauwerkes wird man sich erst bewusst, wenn man den asketischen Innenhof, den größten der Grazer Altstadt, betritt. Besonders eindrucksvoll kommt die Monumentalität beim Durchschreiten der rund um den Innenhof führenden Gänge zum Ausdruck. Stockwerk

gical college of Graz was one of the first of the Society of Jesus in the German countries, and it counted among the largest of the century, along with Augsburg, Munich and Coblenz. While most of the 16th-century colleges were later converted to the Baroque style, the Graz college retained most of its original structural features and is therefore an important example of early Jesuit architecture of significance for the entire German province of the Order. The sheer size of the building registers only on entering the austere inner courtyard, the largest in the historic center of Graz. Passing along the corridors overlooking the courtyard, one gets a particularly vivid impression of its monumentality. Floor upon floor, the long corridors, reminiscent of a monastic cloister, run around the courtyard, willing those who pass to be carried over into a remote world. The attic offers

IV

Priesterseminar, barocke Prunkstiege
Seminary, Baroque grand staircase

um Stockwerk ziehen sich die langen, einem klösterlichen Kreuzgang ähnlichen Gänge um den Hof und scheinen den Durchschreitenden auch heute noch in eine entfernte Welt versetzen zu wollen. Vom Dachgeschoß aus bietet sich ein überwältigender Blick auf das rote Dächermeer von Graz. Während das äußere Erscheinungsbild einen schlichten Renaissancecharakter aufweist, wird die Innenausstattung vom Zeitalter des Barock bestimmt. So stellt neben dem Barocksaal und dem Refektorium vor allem die Prunkstiege das bedeutendste Werk dar, das die Barockzeit im Kollegium hinterlassen hat.

Die Wände des zweiten und dritten Obergeschosses der Prunkstiege erhielten eine farbige Stuccolustro-Verkleidung, die Gewölbefelder der Treppenläufe und des Zwischenpodestes aufwendige Stuckrahmungen mit gemalten Emblemen (kleine symbolhafte Bilder mit Spruchbändern).

an overwhelming view of the red rooftops of Graz. The outward appearance is that of a plain, severe Renaissance building, however the interior is alive with the exuberance of the Baroque age, which left its mark everywhere, and most impressively in the grand hall, the refectory and – first and foremost – the grand staircase.

The walls of the second and third floors were covered in colourful stuccolustro, the severies of the stair flights and the landing were framed in lavish stucco with painted emblems (small symbolic paintings with banderols).

Die alte Jesuitenuniversität

Anschließend an die langgezogene Fassade des Priesterseminars befindet sich der monumentale Baublock der Alten Universität (Bürgergasse 2 a). Dieser bildet die Ecke von der Hofgasse zur Bürgergasse und lässt hier einen kleinen Vorplatz frei, der früher auch Universitätsplatz genannt wurde. Gegenüber fällt der Blick auf die Westfassade des Grazer Domes.

1585 wurde die Universität von Erzherzog Karl II. gegründet, im Jahre 1609 konnte Erzherzog Ferdinand das Gebäude seiner Bestimmung übergeben. Die Auflösung des Jesuitenordens im Jahre 1773 brachte das Ende der Jesuitenuniversität, der Universitätsbetrieb blieb jedoch unter staatlicher Leitung aufrecht.

The Old Jesuit University

The long facade of the seminary abuts the monumental building of the Old University (Bürgergasse 2 a). Placed at the corner of Hofgasse and Bürgergasse, the complex draws back to leave a small square which was once known as University Square. Across the street, the western facade of the cathedral comes into view.

The university was founded by Archduke Charles II in 1585, and the building was ceremonially opened by Archduke Ferdinand in 1609. When the Jesuit order was dissolved in 1773, this spelled the end of the Jesuit university, but operations continued under state control.

Alte Jesuitenuniversität, Bibliothekssaal, Bürgergasse 2 a

Former Jesuit university, library Bürgergasse 2 a

Die Bibliothek

Um die Bücherbestände der aufgehobenen steirischen Jesuitenkollegien (Graz, Leoben, Judenburg) zu sichern, ließ Kaiserin Maria Theresia ab 1780 die ehemalige Aula und das Theater der Universität von Hofbaumeister Jospeh Hueber zu einem prunkvollen Bibliothekssaal umbauen. Die künstlerische Bedeutung des Saales liegt darin, dass Ausstattung und Dekoration vollständig erhalten sind und ein wichtiges Beispiel der Übergangsphase vom Rokoko zum Klassizismus darstellen. Neben Ölgemälden von Jesuitenlehrern und Habsburgerporträts sind Gewölbefelder, Gurten und Fensternischen mit einer zarten Dekorationsmalerei überzogen, in der sich duftige Rokoko-Blüten und klassizistische Vasen harmonisch vereinen und dem Raum seine besondere Note verleihen.

The Library

In order to rescue the library stock of the Styrian Jesuit colleges (Graz, Leoben, Judenburg) after their dissolution, Empress Maria Theresa in 1780 instructed her court builder Joseph Hueber to convert the former aula and theatre of the university into a library, which today is the showpiece of the Styrian archives. The furnishings and decoration of the library have survived fully intact and are a prominent example of the transition period from Rococo to Classicism. The library boasts oil portraits of Jesuit teachers and Habsburg rulers; its severies, transverse arches and window recesses are covered with delicate decorative paintings in which dainty rococo flowers are harmoniously placed in Classicist vases to give the room its special appeal.

IV

Grazer Dom, Westfassade
Cathedral, western facade

Hl. Christophorus, Fresko,
Langschiff, Detailansicht

St. Christopher,
fresco, nave, detail

Der Grazer Dom

Der mächtige gotische Dom ist das Herzstück der Stadtkrone; mit diesem Bau ist auch die Entwicklung der Stadtkrone anzusetzen.
Der Dom wurde unter Kaiser Friedrich III. von 1438 bis 1464 anstelle der 1174 erstmals genannten Pfarrkirche St. Ägydius errichtet. Der gotische Neubau diente weiterhin als Pfarrkirche und wurde in die Stadtbefestigung mit einbezogen.
Am Hauptportal über dem tiefen Gewände des kielbogigen Steintores weisen Wappen auf Friedrich und seine portugiesische Gattin Eleonora hin.
Über dem südlichen Seiteneingang im Inneren der Kirche befindet sich ein fragmentarisches Fresko. Der Heilige Christophorus, der Christus in der Gestalt eines Kindes über den Fluss trägt, zeigt Gesichtszüge Friedrichs mit dem steirischen Herzogshut – zu einem Zeitpunkt, da dieser bereits Kaiser war. Sicher kann darin ein tieferer Sinn gesehen werden, dass Friedrich gerade dem Träger Christi sein Antlitz lieh.
An der südlichen Außenwand des Domes befindet sich das sog. Gottesplagenbild, das vermutlich 1480 von Thomas von Villach geschaffen wurde.
Das Fresko wurde von Grazer Bürgern gestiftet, um Gottes Vergebung für ihre Sündenschuld zu erbitten. Die Strafe Gottes manifestiert sich in den drei Plagen, Heuschrecken, Türken und Pest, im unteren Bildteil. In den oberen Bildteilen zeigen sich göttliche und weltliche Hierarchien in einer wunderbaren Schau. Neben der ältesten Stadtansicht von Graz (oberhalb der Türkenbelagerung) bietet die Darstellung ein im ausgehenden Mittelalter einzigartiges theologisches Programm.
Den entscheidenden Impuls für das Schicksal der Grazer Pfarrkirche löste der Aufstieg

The Cathedral

The mighty Gothic cathedral sits at the heart of the Stadtkrone, and it is this church which is at the root of the Stadtkrone development. Built under Emperor Frederick III in 1438–64, the cathedral replaced the parish church of St. Ägydius, first mentioned in 1174. The new Gothic building continued to serve as the parish church and was incorporated into the city fortifications. The main portal carries the coats of arms of Frederick and Eleonora, his Portuguese wife, above the deep doorcasing of the ogee arch of the stone door.
Inside the southern side entrance, a fragment of a fresco survives showing St. Christopher carrying the Christ child across a river. The saint is clearly recognisable as Frederick wearing the Styrian ducal coronet – at a time when he was already German emperor. There is deep symbolism in the fact that Frederick lent his features to the saint carrying Jesus Christ.
The southern external wall of the Cathedral is decorated with a fresco known as "God's Plagues", probably painted by Thomas von Villach in 1480. It was donated by the burghers of Graz to ask God's forgiveness for their sins. God's punishment had manifested itself in three plagues: locusts, the Turks and the Black Death, depicted in the lower part of the painting. Above it, a marvellous view is given of divine and human hierarchies. The schematic painting, unique for the close of the Middle Ages, also offers the first view of Graz (above the Turkish siege).
The fate of the parish church of Graz was decided when Graz was raised to become the residence of the rulers of Inner Austria in 1564.
Charles II, the Catholic archduke who lived at the Burg from 1564 to 1590, called the

IV

Grazer Dom, gotisches Hauptportal
Cathedral, Gothic main portal

IV

Grazer Dom, Langschiff
Cathedral, nave

von Graz zur Residenzstadt Innerösterreichs im Jahre 1564 aus.

Der katholische Erzherzog Karl II., der von 1564 bis 1590 in der Grazer Burg residierte, berief den Orden der Jesuiten nach Graz, um dem immer stärker werdenden protestantischen Glauben Einhalt zu gebieten.

Zweihundert Jahre lang befand sich die Ägydiuskirche als Zentrum der Gegenreformation unter der Observanz des Jesuitenordens.

In dieser Zeit arbeiteten die besten heimischen und auswärtigen Künstler an der Kirchenausstattung und schufen ein beeindruckendes Gesamtkunstwerk. Päpstliche Schenkungen, wie die kostbaren Reliquienschreine, Meisterwerke der italienischen Frührenaissance, sowie Stiftungen und Epitaphe haben einen hohen Anteil daran. Mit der vom Jesuiten Georg Lindemayr programmatisch festgelegten Kanzel, den Kirchenbänken, dem Chorgestühl und Hauptaltar war die vollständige Barockisierung am Anfang des 18. Jahrhunderts im Wesentlichen abgeschlossen, die gegenwärtig den prunkvollen Kirchenraum prägt.

1773 wurde der Jesuitenorden durch Papst Clemens XIV. aus politischen Gründen aufgehoben. Als im Zuge der josefinischen Diözesanregulierung 1786 der Bischofsitz von Graz nach Seckau verlegt wurde, bot sich die nur von einigen ehemaligen Jesuiten betreute Ägydiuskirche an.

Die ursprüngliche Pfarrkirche, später Hof- und Jesuitenkirche St. Ägydius, war somit Dom der Diözese Graz-Seckau geworden.

Society of Jesus to Graz in order to check the progress made by the Protestant religion. For 200 years the Church of St. Ägydius was controlled by the Jesuits as the centre of the Counter-Reformation.

During this period, the best local and foreign artists put their efforts into furnishing the church, creating an impressive Gesamtkunstwerk. Gifts by the Styrian prince, such as the precious reliquaries, masterpieces of early Italian Renaissance, foundations and epitaphs also contributed their share. The pulpit, whose programme was devised by Georg Lindemayr of the Society of Jesus, the pews, choir stalls and high altar essentially achieved the transformation into the Baroque style in the early 18th century which today defines the character of the magnificent interior.

In 1773, Pope Clement XIV suppressed the Jesuit order for political reasons. When Joseph II revised the scheme of dioceses in 1786, moving the bishop's seat from Seckau to Graz, the church of St. Ägydius, attended by only a handful of former Jesuits, was ideally placed to become the new cathedral of the diocese of Graz-Seckau. In this way, a parish church turned court church and then Jesuit church was at last raised to cathedral status.

IV

Mausoleum, Fassade mit Katharinenkirche

Mausoleum, facade, St. Catherine's Church

Das Mausoleum Kaiser Ferdinands II.

Das Mausoleum mit der Katharinenkirche (1614–1687) stellt den architektonisch und kunsthistorisch interessantesten Baukomplex der Stadtkrone dar. Erweisen sich die Gesamtanlage und die markante Fassade als einzigartige Dokumente einer Baugesinnung an der Wende von der Renaissance zum Barock, so ist es vor allem die weit sichtbare Kuppellandschaft, die dem Stadtbild die charakteristische Silhouette verleiht.

Mit dem Baukomplex der Katharinenkirche und dem über ovalem Grundriss errichteten Mausoleum – dem größten Mausoleumsbau der Habsburger – entstand ein imperiales Bauwerk, dessen kunstgeschichtliche Bedeutung in seiner einzigartigen Synthese von

The Mausoleum of Emperor Ferdinand II

The Mausoleum and St. Catherine's Church (1614–87) contribute the most interesting – in terms of architecture and art history – components to the Stadtkrone. While the overall design of the complex and the striking façade are unique indicators of an architectural fashion at the threshold of the Renaissance and Baroque, it is the characteristic domescape that lends the city's silhouette its distinctive touch.

The Mausoleum, placed on an oval groundplan and the Habsburgs' largest tomb, together with St. Catherine's provides an imperial edifice whose important place in art history derives from its unique synthesis of heavy, moulded architecture and the soaring,

IV

Mausoleum, Gruftraum
Mausoleum, tomb

schwerer plastisch durchgearbeiteter Architektur mit einer von Venedig inspirierten leichten Kuppellandschaft liegt. Im Detail dem Manierismus verhaftet, nimmt die Gesamtanlage bereits barocke Elemente vorweg.

Für den Bau seines Mausoleums verpflichtete Erzherzog Ferdinand den aus der Lombardei stammenden Giovanni Pietro de Pomis, der sich in Graz auch als Architekt bewährte und zum Hofbaumeister avancierte.

Das Bauwerk des Mausoleums bilden zwei miteinander verbundene, in ihrem Raumkonzept jedoch verschiedene Gebäude; das heißt: eine der hl. Katharina geweihte Kirche über kreuzförmigem Grundriss und das eigentliche Mausoleum als ovaler Zentralbau. Der traditionellen kreuzförmigen Kirchenanlage steht damit ein Zentralbau gegenüber, dessen ovaler Grundrisstypus

Venice-inspired lightness of its domes. Rooted in Mannerism in its details, the complex nevertheless anticipates various elements of the new Baroque style.

For his Mausoleum, Archduke Ferdinand retained Giovanni Pietro de Pomis from Lombardy, who proved to be a skilled architect and rose to become court builder.

The complex consists of two buildings which are linked but differ in their uses: a church dedicated to St. Catherine above a cruciform ground plan, and the mausoleum proper, a centralised, oval building. In this way, the traditional cross-shaped church is juxtaposed with a centrally designed building whose oval base design was only just gaining ground in Italy and which was a striking novelty in northern architecture.

With only a small passage left between, the church, distinguished by its characteristic

in Italien erst allmählich durchzusetzen begann und für die nördliche Architektur eine völlige Novität darstellte.

Nur einen schmalen Durchgang freilassend, fand die Kirche mit der charakteristischen Fassade neben der Ägydiuskirche ihren Platz.

Für den Mausoleumsbau, der sich aus einem mächtig aufragenden Kuppelraum und dem darunter liegenden Gruftraum zusammensetzt, nützte de Pomis das steile Terrain geschickt aus. Diese bewußt genutzte Geländestufe zwingt den Besucher von der Helligkeit der Kirche in das Dunkel des stuckierten Gruftraumes hinabzusteigen. Damit ist das Thema der wirkungsvollen Rauminszenierung, ein wesentlicher Bestandteil des Barock in unseren Breiten, um Jahrzehnte vorausgestaltet.

Neben den vielgerühmten Kuppeln, die an Pietro de Pomis Lehrjahre in Italien denken lassen, ist es vor allem die Mausoleumsfassade, die das besondere Interesse weckt und den von Dom und Domherrenhof flankierten Platz prägt.

Unzählige Maler und Fotografen hielten sie im Bilde fest, viele Publikationen setzten sich mit der Fülle ihrer architektonischen Details auseinander.

In diesem Zusammenhang muss erwogen werden, dass sich de Pomis als genialer Universalkünstler sehr wohl einer städtebaulichen Komponente bewusst war.

Die am anderen Murufer gelegene Mariahilferkirche war wie Venedigs Inselkirche San Giorgio Maggiore auf Fernwirkung berechnet, dagegen ist die ausgeführte Mausoleumsfassade mit ihrem kleinteiligen, malerischen Ausdruck ganz offensichtlich auf eine den damaligen Gegebenheiten entsprechende Nahsichtigkeit ausgerichtet.

Die triumphbogenartig konzipierte Fassade facade, fits tightly up against the Cathedral. For the Mausoleum, which consists of a dynamic rising domed structure and a tomb underneath, de Pomis made skilful use of the precipitous terrain. Exploiting the natural terrace, he forces visitors to descend from the brightness of the church into the gloom of the stuccoed tomb, thereby anticipating the art of effective stage-setting, a key element of the Baroque in Central Europe, by decades.

Apart from the famous and acclaimed domes, which echo de Pomis' apprenticeship in Italy, it is mostly the facade of the Mausoleum which excites special interest and which dominates the square flanked by the cathedral and the Domherrenhof. Innumerable painters and photographers have captured the image, countless publications have dwelled on the richness of its architectural detail.

In this connection it should be noted that de Pomis, a genius and universal artist, consciously planned the visual impact of his building on the urban environment. The Mariahilferkirche on the opposite bank of the river Mur had been designed for its distant effect, like the Venetian island church San Giorgio Maggiore, while the Mausoleum facade, with its wealth of fine details, obviously was designed for closer viewing.

Resembling a triumphal arch in concept, the facade rises on half columns towards an attic terminated by a segmental arch pediment, inscribed with a triangular pediment – a motif taken from the Jesuits' founding church Il Gesù in Rome. The overwhelming wealth of architectural details ranks the facade foremost among the Mannerist church facades in Austria.

When Ferdinand moved to Vienna in 1619, construction work faltered. After de Pomis' death in 1633, his successor Pietro Valnegro

IV

zeigt über den Halbsäulen ein Attikageschoß mit abschließendem Segmentbogengiebel, dem ein Dreieckgiebel eingeschreiben ist, ein Motiv der Jesuiten-Mutterkirche Il Gesù in Rom.

Die Fülle der architektonischen Einzelformen weist die Fassade als bedeutendste manieristische Kirchenfassade Österreichs aus. Nachdem Ferdinand 1619 nach Wien übersiedelt war, geriet der Bau ins Stocken. Als de Pomis 1633 verstarb, vollendete dessen Nachfolger Pietro Valnegro den Chorturm. 1637 verstarb Kaiser Ferdinand II. in Wien. 320 Reiter begleiteten den kaiserlichen Leichenzug bis zur steirischen Grenze. Nach tagelangen Trauerzeremonien wurde Ferdinand im Mausoleum seiner Geburtsstadt Graz zur letzten Ruhe gebettet. Die Grabstätte ist durch eine schlichte Inschrifttafel rechts vom Altar gekennzeichnet. Das Zentrum des Gruftraumes nimmt ein kostbarer Rotmarmor-Sarkophag ein, darauf die Liegefiguren von Erzherzog Karl II. von Innerösterreich und seiner Gattin Maria von Bayern. Die Raumdekoration zeigt eine von Vergänglichkeitssymbolen geprägte Stuckierung. Keines der Mausoleen, die sich ein Mitglied des Hauses Habsburg errichten hat lassen, übertrifft in Größe und Aussage den Grazer Bau. In ihm konnte sich Ferdinand verewigen, der vom Papst den Ehrentitel „feurigster Verteidiger des katholischen Glaubens" erhalten hatte. Insofern ist der Mausoleumsbau auch als das kunst- und kulturgeschichtlich bedeutendste Baudenkmal der Gegenreformation in der 1. Hälfte des 17. Jahrhunderts in Österreich zu werten. Den prunkvollen Glanzpunkt im Innenraum der mit habsburgischen Apotheosemotiven stuckierten Katharinenkirche setzt der in Graz geborene berühmte Barockbaumeister Fischer von Erlach mit dem Katharinenaltar, dem ersten Meisterwerk in seiner Heimatstadt Graz.

completed the choir tower. In 1637, Ferdinand, the second emperor of this name in Germany, died in Vienna. His funeral procession was accompanied to the Styrian border by 320 horsemen. After days of funeral ceremonies, Ferdinand was at last laid to rest in the Mausoleum of his native town. His grave is indicated by a plain tablet to the right of the altar. The vault itself is dominated by a precious sarcophagus of red marble, with statues of Archduke Charles II of Inner Austria and his wife Maria of Bavaria placed on top. The room is decorated with stucco redolent with symbols of the transience of life.

None of the mausoleums erected by the various members of the Habsburg dynasty surpasses that in Graz for sheer size and expressiveness. Ferdinand, whom the pope had awarded the honorary title of "most fervent defender of the faith", used it as an opportunity to immortalise himself. As such, the building should also be seen as Austria's most important monument, in terms of art and culture, of the Counter-Reformation in the first half of the 17th century.

Inside St. Catherine's, stuccoed all over in motifs glorifying the Habsburgs, the most splendid item is the altar created by Fischer von Erlach, a native of Graz who went on to become a leading exponent of the Baroque style. It was the first masterpiece that the architect was to give his home town.

The Application of the City of Graz

Die Bewerbung der Stadt Graz

V

The Application of the City of Graz

Die Bewerbung der Stadt Graz

Dieser Bericht soll einen summarischen Überblick zu den wichtigsten Fakten des UNESCO-Projektes Grazer Altstadt bieten und einen Einblick in die spezifischen Bewerbungsgrundlagen ermöglichen.

Die Realisierung dieses Vorhabens beruhte auf dem komplexen Zusammenspiel der zuständigen Behörden der Stadt Graz mit den entsprechenden Institutionen in Wien und Paris.

This report gives a summary overview of the most important facts about the UNESCO project and the old town of Graz, and an insight into the specific application principles.

The realization of this project was based on complex co-operation between the responsible authorities of the city of Graz and corresponding institutions in Vienna and Paris.

DIE UNESCO-KONVENTION

Das Natur- und Kulturerbe der Menschheit ist durch Ausbeutung von Ressourcen, Umweltzerstörung, kriegerische Auseinandersetzungen und Naturkatastrophen äußerst gefährdet. Um der Bedrohung dieses Erbes entgegenzuwirken, wurde 1972 die UNESCO-Konvention zum Schutz des Kultur- und Naturerbes der Welt beschlossen. Bis heute haben 118 Staaten (Stand 2000) die Welterbekonvention unterzeichnet. 1993 trat Österreich diesem wichtigen Übereinkommen bei und hat bisher fünf Welterbestätten – **Schloss Schönbrunn, Altstadt von Salzburg, Region Hallstatt, Semmeringbahn und die Altstadt von Graz** – vorzuweisen.

THE UNESCO CONVENTION

Mankind's natural and cultural heritage is at extreme risk from exploitation of resources, environmental destruction, wars and natural disasters. In order to counter this threat to our heritage, in 1972 the UNESCO Convention for the Protection of the World Cultural and Natural Heritage was agreed. To this day, 118 states (as of 2000) have signed the World Heritage Convention. Austria joined into this important agreement in 1993 and now has five world heritage sites: **Schloss Schönbrunn, the historic city of Salzburg, the region of Hallstatt, the Semmering railway and the historic city of Graz.**

Das Welterbe-Komitee und die Welterbeliste

Tritt ein Staat der Welterbe-Konvention bei, kann er besondere Natur- und Kulturgüter innerhalb seiner Landesgrenzen für die Aufnahme in die Welterbeliste vorschlagen. Diese Natur- und Kulturdenkmäler müssen von außergewöhnlichem Wert sein und den Kriterien der Einzigartigkeit und Authentizität entsprechen. Die diesbezügliche Prüfung wird vom zwischenstaatlichen Welterbe-Komitee vorgenommen, das sich aus Experten von 21 Mitgliedstaaten zusammensetzt, die über die Aufnahme in die Welterbeliste entscheiden. Beraten wird das Welterbe-Komitee von der IUCN (Internationale Union zum Schutz der Natur) und dem ICOMOS (Internationaler Rat für Denkmalpflege). Eine dritte Organisation, das Internationale Studienzentrum für die Erhaltung und Restaurierung von Kulturgut (ICCROM, Rom-Zentrum für die Ausbildung von Fachkräften), berät das Komitee in Fragen der Restaurierung und der Ausbildung von entsprechenden Fachkräften.

The World Heritage Committee and the World Heritage List

When a state joins the World Heritage Convention, it may nominate certain natural and cultural properties within its borders for inscription on the World Heritage List. These natural and cultural sites must be of outstanding value and meet certain criteria of uniqueness and authenticity. A corresponding assessment is carried out by the International World Heritage Committee, consisting of experts from 21 member states, who decide whether it should be inscribed on the World Heritage List. The World Heritage Committee receives consultation from the IUCN (International Union for Conservation of Nature and Natural Resources) and the ICOMOS (International Council of Monuments and Sites). A third organization, the International Centre for the Study of the Preservation and Restoration of Cultural Property (ICCROM) advises the jury regarding renovation and the training of appropriate specialists.

Auswahlkriterien

Um in die Welterbeliste aufgenommen zu werden, muss ein Natur- oder Kulturgut gewisse Bedingungen erfüllen, wobei folgende sechs Kriterien für Kulturgüter maßgebend sind:

Das Objekt
1 | ist eine einzigartige künstlerische Leistung, ein Meisterwerk des schöpferischen Geistes.
2 | hat während einer Zeitspanne oder in einem Kulturgebiet der Erde beträchtlichen Einfluss auf die Entwicklung der Architektur, der Großplastik oder des Städtebaus und der Landschaftsgestaltung ausgeübt.
3 | stellt ein einzigartiges oder zumindest ein außergewöhnliches Zeugnis einer untergegangenen Zivilisation oder Kulturtradition dar.
4 | ist ein herausragendes Beispiel eines Typus von Gebäuden oder architektonischen Ensembles oder einer Landschaft und stellt bedeutsame Abschnitte in der menschlichen Geschichte dar.
5 | stellt ein hervorragendes Beispiel einer überlieferten menschlichen Siedlungsform oder Landnutzung dar, die für eine bestimmte Kultur typisch ist, insbesondere, wenn sie unter dem Druck unaufhaltsamen Wandels vom Untergang bedroht wird.
6 | ist in unmittelbarer oder erkennbarer Weise mit Ereignissen, lebendigen Traditionen, mit Ideen oder Glaubensbekenntnissen, mit künstlerischen oder literarischen Werken von außergewöhnlicher universeller Bedeutung verknüpft.

Die historische Echtheit eines Denkmals sowie die Qualität der Schutz- und Erhaltungsmaßnahmen sind von gleichrangiger Bedeutung.

Die für die Aufnahme in die Weltkulturerbeliste erforderliche Beschreibung der Kultur- oder Naturgüter hat nach einem vorgegebenen Bewerbungsformular zu erfolgen (Format for the nomination of cultural and natural properties for the inscription of the World Heritage List).
Diese Kriterien liegen als Richtlinien für die Anwendung der World Heritage Konvention zugrunde.

Selection Criteria

In order to be included in the World Heritage List, natural or cultural properties must fulfil certain criteria, whereby the following six criteria are applicable for cultural assets:

Each property nominated should:
1 | represent a masterpiece of human creative genius; or
2 | exhibit an important interchange of human values, over a span of time or within a cultural area of the world, of developments in architectures or technology, monumental arts, town-planning or landscape design; or
3 | bear a unique or at least exceptional testimony to a cultural tradition or to a civilization which is living or which has disappeared; or
4 | be an outstanding example of a type of building or architectural or technological ensemble or landscape which illustrates (a) significant stage(s) in human history; or
5 | be an outstanding example of a traditional human settlement or land-use which is representative of a culture (or cultures), especially when it has become vulnerable under the impact of irreversible change; or
6 | be directly or tangibly associated with events or living traditions, with ideas, or with beliefs, with artistic and literary works of outstanding universal significance.

The historical authenticity of the monument and the quality of the measures of preservation and upkeep are of equal importance.

The description of the cultural and natural properties required for inclusion in the World Heritage List must be carried out according to a specified application form (Format for the nomination of cultural and natural properties for inscription on the World Heritage List).
These criteria serve as indicators for the Operational Guidelines for the Implementation of the World Heritage Convention.

V

Format

1 | Identifikation des Kulturgutes. Allgemeine Daten
a   Land (Landesteil, wenn unterschiedlich)
b   Bundesstaat, Bundesland oder Region
c   Name des Kulturgutes
d   Genaue Position auf der Karte und Angabe der geographischen Koordinaten zur nächsten Sekunde
e   Karten und/oder Pläne mit den Grenzen der für die Aufnahme vorgeschlagenen Gebiete und aller Pufferzonen
f   Ausmaß des für die Eintragung vorgeschlagenen Gebietes und der Pufferzone, falls vorhanden

2 | Rechtfertigung für die Eintragung
a   Darstellung der Bedeutung
b   Mögliche vergleichende Analyse (inkl. Erhaltungszustand vergleichbarer Kulturgüter)
c   Authentizität/Integrität
d   Kriterien, nach welchen die Eintragung vorgeschlagen wurde (und Rechtfertigung für die Eintragung nach diesen Kriterien)

3 | Beschreibung
a   Beschreibung des Kulturgutes
b   Geschichte und Entwicklung
c   Gestalt und Daten der jüngsten Aufzeichnungen über das Kulturgut
d   Derzeitiger Erhaltungszustand
e   Vorgangsweise und Programme für die Präsentation von dem und Werbung für das Kulturgut

4 | Verwaltung
a   Eigentümer
b   Rechtlicher Status
c   Schutzmaßnahmen und Mittel zur Durchsetzung derselben
d   Agentur/en mit Verwaltungsbefugnissen
e   Verwaltungsebene (z. B. ad Kulturgut oder ad Region) sowie Name und Adresse der für Kontakte zuständigen Person
f   Pläne betreffend das Kulturgut (z. B. regionale und lokale Pläne, Erhaltungsprogramm, Entwicklungsplan für Tourismus)
g   Finanzierungsquellen und Ausmaß

Format

1 | Identification of the Property, General data
a   Country (and State Party if different)
b   State, Province or Region
c   Name of Property
d   Exact location on map and indication of geographical coordinates to the nearest second
e   Maps/and or plans showing boundary of area proposed for inscription and of any buffer zone
f   Area of property proposed for inscription and proposed buffer zone if any

2 | Justification for Inscription
a   Statement of significance
b   Possible comparative analysis (including state of conservation of similar properties)
c   Authenticity/Integrity
d   Criteria under which inscription is proposed (and justification for inscription under these criteria)

3 | Description
a   Description of Property
b   History and Development
c   Form and date of most recent records of property
d   Present state of conservation
e   Policies and programmes related to the presentation and promotion of the property

4 | Management
a   Ownership
b   Legal status
c   Protective measures and means of implementing them
d   Agency/agencies with management authority
e   Level at which management is exercised (e.g. on property, regionally) and name and address of responsible person for contact purposes
f   Agreed plans relating to property (e.g. regional, local plan, conservation plan, tourism development plan)
g   Sources and levels of finance

h	Quellen über Sachkenntnisse und Ausbildungsniveau im Bereich Erhaltungstechniken und Verwaltung	h	Sources of expertise and training in conservation and management techniques
i	Einrichtungen für Besucher und Statistiken	i	Visitor facilities and statistics
j	Verwaltungsplan für das Kulturgut und Zielkatalog	j	Property management plan and statement of objectives
k	Qualifikation des Personals (professionell/technische Wartung)	k	Staffing levels (professional, technical, maintenance)

5 | Faktoren, die sich auf das Kulturgut auswirken
a Druck von außen
(z. B. bauliche Eingriffe, Adaption, Landwirtschaft, Bergbau)
b Umwelteinflüsse (z. B. Luftverschmutzung, Klimawechsel)
c Naturkatastrophen und entsprechende Vorbeugungsmaßnahmen (Erdbeben, Hochwasser, Feuer etc.)
d Druck durch Besucher und Touristen
e Anzahl der Bewohner innerhalb des Kulturgutes (Gebäudes), Pufferzone
f Andere

5 | Factors affecting the property
a Development pressures
(e.g. encroachment, adaptation, agriculture, mining)
b Environmental pressures (e.g. pollution, climate change)
c Natural disasters and precautions
(earthquakes, floods, fires, etc.)
d Visitor/tourism pressures
e Number of inhabitants within property, buffer zone
f Other

6 | Überwachung
a Schlüsselindikatoren zur Beurteilung des Erhaltungszustandes
b Verwaltungsmaßnahmen zur Überwachung des Kulturgutes
c Ergebnisse früherer Berichte

6 | Monitoring
a Key indicators for measuring state of conservation
b Administrative arrangements for monitoring property
c Results of previous reporting exercises

7 | Dokumentation
a Fotos, Dias und, wenn verfügbar, Film- oder Videomaterial
b Kopien der Verwaltungsunterlagen und Auszüge anderer Pläne über das Kulturgut
c Bibliographie
d Adresse an der das Inventar, Aufzeichnungen und das Archiv verwaltet werden

7 | Documentation
a Photographs, slides and, where available, film/video
b Copies of property management plans and extracts of other plans relevant to the property
c Bibliography
d Address where inventory, records and archives are held

BEWERBUNGSGRUNDLAGEN ZUR AUFNAHME DER STADT GRAZ IN DIE WELTKULTURERBELISTE GEMÄSS DER UNESCO-KONVENTION

Folgende Unterlagen wurden eingereicht:
Dokumentation Altstadt Graz (50 Seiten Text, 50 Fotos)
50 Dias
Österreichisches Denkmalschutzgesetz
Grazer Altstadterhaltungsgesetz
Kunsttopographie Graz-Altstadt

APPLICATION PRINCIPLES FOR THE INSCRIPTION OF THE CITY OF GRAZ ON THE WORLD HERITAGE LIST ACCORDING TO THE UNESCO CONVENTION

The following documents were submitted:
Documentation of the Old Town (50 pages text, 50 photographs)
50 Slides
Austrian Law on Monument Protection
Graz Law on the Preservation of the Historic Center
Art Topography Graz – Historic Center

Format: Antragsformular

1 | Identifikation des Kulturgutes

a | Österreich
b | Bundesland Steiermark
c | Graz – Altstadt
d | siehe Dokumentation
e | siehe Dokumentation
f | siehe Dokumentation

2 | Rechtfertigung für die Eintragung

a | Das historische Zentrum von Graz repräsentiert mit der Geschlossenheit seiner vielschichtigen Bausubstanz vom Mittelalter bis in das 19. Jahrhundert und deren hervorragender Erhaltung ein singuläres Denkmal einer historischen Stadt im zentraleuropäischen Raum. Die weder durch Krieg noch durch Wirtschaftswunder-Einbrüche beeinträchtigte Authentizität des gewachsenen Zustandes und seiner überlieferten Erscheinung wird hier exemplarisch veranschaulicht.

In der engen Verbundenheit von Fluss und Schlossberg entstand seit dem Mittelalter ein Stadtorganismus, der späterhin als Residenz und als Bollwerk des Reiches gegen die Osmanen jahrhundertelang eine wichtige europäische Mission erfüllte. Klar und lückenlos wie kaum sonstwo spiegelt sich im Stadtbild bis heute die Entwicklungsgeschichte wider. Jede Epoche ist mit charakteristischen Gruppen von Baudenkmälern vertreten, die, einander ergänzend, sich zu einem geschlossenen Gesamtbild einer unversehrt erhaltenen Altstadt zusammenfügen. Eine einzigartige Mischung mediterraner und nördlicher Elemente aus dem weitgespannten Zusammenhang der Österreichisch-Ungarischen Monarchie, die Vermengung von Kultureinflüssen zwischen Adria, Donauraum und dem Balkan prägen bis heute die Atmosphäre der Stadt. Dies kommt in der Stadtstruktur, im Stimmungswert der Straßen, Plätze und schmalen Gassen ebenso zum Ausdruck wie im architektonischen Formenreichtum der Kirchen, Klöster, Paläste und Bürgerhäuser. Die Erweiterung der Stadt im 19. und 20. Jahrhundert hat ihr historisches Gepräge noch akzentuiert, indem sie die Altstadt durch einen Grüngürtel im Bereich der ehemals großangelegten nachmittelalterlichen Befestigungen umrahmte.

Format: Application Form

1 | Identification of the Property

a | Austria
b | Federal province of Styria
c | Graz – historic center
d | see documentation
e | see documentation
f | see documentation

2 | Justification for Inscription

a | Owing to its ensemble of buildings from many periods (from the Middle Ages up to the 19th century), excellently preserved in its entirety and integrity, the historic center of Graz represents a singular monument of a historic Central-European town. The authenticity of its evolved state and traditional appearance, unharmed by wars or post-war economic boom times, is shown here in an exemplary manner.

Between the river and Schlossberg an urban organism emerged from the Middle Ages onward that was to fulfil an important European mission later on as a court residence and stronghold of the empire against the Ottomans. Hardly anywhere else is a history of development mirrored in the townscape so clearly and completely. Each period is represented by characteristic groups of architectural monuments that complement each other and come together in a uniform whole as an intact historic center. To this day, the atmosphere of the city is characterised by a unique mix of Mediterranean and northern elements from the wide expanse of the Austro-Hungarian Monarchy, to the mingling of cultural influences from the regions between the Adriatic Sea, the Danube, and the Balkans. All of this finds its expression in the structure of the city, the atmosphere of its streets, squares and narrow lanes, and in the wealth of architectural form found in its churches, monasteries, palaces and burgher houses. The extension of the city in the 19th and 20th centuries has added to this historic impression by encircling the historic center with a green belt on the site of the former large-scale post-medieval fortifications. The social structure of the historic center with its acceptance of traditional living space within the confines of the historic building ensemble has also been preserved to a high degree.

Auch die soziale Struktur der Altstadt mit der Akzeptanz des traditionellen Lebensraumes im historischen Baugefüge blieb weitgehend erhalten.

Das Mittelalter hinterließ mächtige Hallenkirchen und die städtische Grundstruktur mit ihren dicht gedrängten Bürgerhäusern zu Füßen des Schlossberges und zu beiden Seiten des Flusses. Aus der Renaissance- und Barockzeit ist eine große Zahl prominenter Sakralbauten, stattlicher Stadtpalais, stimmungsvoller Arkadenhöfe und prächtiger Fassaden überliefert. Zuletzt umgab die klassizistische Epoche den Altstadtkörper an dessen Süd- und Ostseite mit weitläufigen Gebäudefronten. Der exemplarische Erhaltungszustand von Stadtstruktur und Stadtbild in der überlieferten Erscheinung spiegelt bis heute in der Kontinuität der sozialen Konkordanz auch die wirtschafts- und gesellschaftspolitische Entwicklung und Stellung der Stadt wider. Insgesamt kommt dem historischen Zentrum von Graz daher außergewöhnlicher Wert zu: als spezifischer Typus eines Stadtdenkmals ebenso wie als überlieferter baulicher Zusammenhang in einem exzeptionellen Erhaltungszustand.

b | Das historische Zentrum von Graz ist in seinem architektonisch geschlossenen Erhaltungszustand anderen Altstädten nicht leicht gegenüberzustellen.
Am ehesten vergleichbar ist die Altstadt von Graz noch mit Bern hinsichtlich der geschlossenen Dichte der historischen Bausubstanz und des unversehrt erhaltenen Gesamtzusammenhanges.

c | Das historische Zenturm von Graz ist als signifikantes Dokument für den Begriff Urbanität zu bezeichnen. Authentizität ist nicht nur im geschlossenen historischen Baubestand, sondern auch in den in vielen Bauten einander überlagernden Bauphasen vom Mittelalter bis in die Neuzeit, im Nebeneinander unterschiedlicher stilistischer Elemente sowie im Bewusstsein der Bevölkerung einer langen Tradition als Teil des Heute gegeben. Identität von Tradition und aktueller, lebendiger Funktion bestimmt die einmalig Synthese dieser Stadt. Die unversehrte Erhaltung der Baudenkmäler erfolgt daher nicht nur durch die Denkmalpflege, sondern ist vor allem durch das seit Generationen gegebene Selbstverständnis der Eigentümer in der Akzeptanz dieser Authentizität gewährleistet.

The Middle Ages left mighty hall churches as well as the basic urban structure with its tightly-packed burgher houses at the foot of the Schlossberg and along both sides of the river. The Renaissance and Baroque periods are represented by a large number of ecclesiastical structures, the imposing townhouses of the aristocracy, idyllic arcaded courtyards and splendid facades. Finally, the Classicist period surrounded the southern and eastern parts of the historic center with an extensive array of buildings. Owing to their exemplary state of preservation, the urban structure and townscape and their traditional appearance still reflect the economic and sociopolitical development and status of the city with its continuity of social consensus. Thus the historic center of Graz as a whole is of outstanding value: both as a specific type of urban monument and as an exceptionally well-preserved traditional architectural ensemble.

b | Due to the architectural integrity of its state of preservation, it is difficult to compare the historic center of Graz with other historic centers. The most likely parallel is probably Bern with its compact integrity of historic building material and generally intact prospect.

c | The historic center of Graz constitutes a significant document for the concept of urbanity. Its authenticity is expressed not only in the integrity of the historic building material, but also in many buildings that combine features of architectural periods ranging from the Middle Ages up to modern times, in the co-existence of various stylistic elements and in the awareness of its inhabitants of a long tradition that forms part of contemporary everyday life. The identity of tradition and modern living functionality determines the unique synthesis of this city. Therefore the conservation of historic monuments is being carried out not only by the authorities concerned but primarily by the owners themselves, whose acceptance of this authenticity has been passed down from generation to generation.

d | Kriterium IV (Die Altstadt von Graz ist ein außergewöhnliches Beispiel eines architektonischen Ensembles, das bedeutende Momente der Geschichte der Menschheit dokumentiert.)
Die Altstadt von Graz zählt in ihrer baulichen Geschlossenheit sowie in der Vielfalt der in ihr vertretenen architektonischen Stilepochen zu einem der schönsten und bedeutendsten Stadtdenkmälern Europas.

Klar und lückenlos, wie kaum anderswo, spiegelt sich im Stadtbild seine Entwicklungsgeschichte wider. Jede Stilphase ist mit charakteristischen, qualitätsvollen Gruppen von Baudenkmälern vertreten, die, einander ergänzend, sich zu einem einheitlichen geschlossenen Ganzen zusammenfügen, dominiert vom hochaufragenden Schlossberg, malerisch durchflossen vom Fluss Mur.

3 | Beschreibung

a | siehe Dokumentation

b | siehe Dokumentation

c | Die Kunstdenkmäler der Stadt Graz,
Die Profanbauten des I. Bezirkes, Altstadt,
Österreichische Kunsttopographie, Bd. LIII, Wien 1997
DEHIO-Handbuch, Die Kunstdenkmäler Österreichs, Graz,
bearbeitet von Horst Schweigert, Wien 1979
Weitere aktuelle Publikationen zur Stadtgeschichte

d | Den gesamten Baubestand in Zone und Pufferzone kennzeichnet eine exzeptionelle Erhaltung des gewachsenen Zustandes, d. h. aller darin inbegriffener historischer Schichten. Dies kommt im Erscheinungsbild der Plätze und Straßen, der Fassaden und Höfe und insbesondere auch in der einmalig unversehrt erhaltenen Dachlandschaft anschaulich zum Ausdruck. Der gute Erhaltungszustand umfasst, über die Baudenkmäler und ihren architekturgeschichtlich wertvollen Details hinaus, auch das Ambiente der historischen Bausubstanz.

e | Eine engagierte Kulturpolitik der Stadt trägt seit langem zur Erhaltung des historischen Stadtzentrums bei, indem alle wichtigen kulturellen Veranstaltungen die historische Altstadt miteinbeziehen.

d | Criterion IV (The historic center of Graz is an outstanding example of an architectural ensemble which illustrates significant stages in human history.)
With its unspoilt integrity and wide variety of architectural styles, the historic center of Graz is among the most beautiful and important urban monuments in Europe.

In a clear and complete way which is virtually unparalleled in any other city, the townscape mirrors directly its history of development. Each architectural period is represented by characteristic high-quality groups of buildings that complement each other to make a uniform whole, its atmosphere dominated by the majestic Schlossberg and the picturesque Mur river.

3 | Description

a | see documentation

b | see documentation

c | Die Kunstdenkmäler der Stadt Graz,
Die Profanbauten des I. Bezirkes, Altstadt,
Österreichische Kunsttopographie, Bd. LIII, Wien 1997
DEHIO-Handbuch, Die Kunstdenkmäler Österreichs, Graz,
edited by Horst Schweigert, Wien 1979
Further relevant publications on the history of the city.

d | All of the building material in the zone and buffer zone is characterised by an exceptional preservation of its evolved state, i.e. of all its historic strata. This is vividly illustrated by the squares and streets, facades and courtyards, and particularly by the uniquely preserved roofscape. This superb state of preservation includes not only the architectural monuments with their historically valuable details, but also the whole ambience of the historic building material.

e | The active cultural policy pursued by the municipality has for a long time contributed to the preservation of the historic center by including it in all important cultural events.

Aktuelle Aktivitäten:
Für die Restaurierung von Fassaden wurden die Altstadtfondsmittel von 2,2 auf 4,4 Millionen Schilling verdoppelt; für die Sanierung des Stadtparks sind 17,6 Millionen Schilling vorgesehen.
Geplante Maßnahmen im Blickwinkel „Graz – Kulturhauptstadt Europa 2003":
Sanierung der Parkanlagen bis 2003 (Kosten ca. 100 Millionen Schilling).
Konzept „Platz für Menschen" – Gestaltung von Plätzen und Straßenzügen der Altstadt im Sinne der Stadterhaltungspflege (1998: Schwerpunkt Sporgasse, Kosten 1,5 Millionen Schilling); 1999: Im Rahmen des EU-Projektes URBAN: Griesplatz Nord, Kosten ca. 10 Millionen Schilling; bis 2001: Griesplatz Süd, Kosten ca. 70 Millionen Schilling).
Wohnsitzinitiative zur Belebung der Altstadt.
Künftige städtische Investitionen im Sanierungsbereich Rathaus und Amtshaus (Kosten ca. 120 Millionen Schilling).
Ausbau einer Kulturachse (Eisernes Haus, Mariahilferplatz/Kulturzentrum Minoriten, Schlossbergstollen, Universitäts-Campus, Glashäuser/Botanischer Garten).
Schlossberg:
Sanierung und bauliche Aufwertung: Uhrturm mit Vorplatz, Glockenturm, Kasematten, Chinesischer Pavillon, Stollen, Wegsicherung (Kosten ca. 45 Millionen Schilling), Cerrini-Schlössl und Starcke-Häuschen (Kosten ca. 11 Millionen Schilling), Wege und Parkanlagen (ca. 20 Millionen Schilling).

4 | Verwaltung

a | Das historische Stadtzentrum in der für die World Heritage List vorgeschlagenen Zone umfaßt 450 Baudenkmäler.
Der Großteil befindet sich im Privatbesitz von seit vielen Generationen hier ansässigen Familien, deren Traditionsbewusstsein die unversehrte Erhaltung dieser Bauwerke gewährleistet. Darüberhinaus ist eine umfassende legal protection gesichert. Diese gilt auch für zahlreiche Gebäude im Eigentum der Republik Österreich, des Landes Steiermark und der Stadt Graz oder anderer öffentlich-rechtlicher Körperschaften sowie der gesetzlich anerkannten Kirchen.

b | Zur Bewahrung des historischen Zentrums von Graz existieren mehrere einander überlagernde Schutzebenen:

Current activities:
The funds allocated for the historic center were doubled from ATS 2.2 to 4.4 million in order to finance the restoration of facades. ATS 17.6 million have been set aside for the renovation of the City Park.
Measures planned for the "Graz – Cultural Capital of Europe 2003" project:
Concept "Platz für Menschen" (Room for People), designing of squares and streets in the historic center within the scope of city conversation of the EU project URBAN: Griesplatz North, approximate costs ATS 70 million).
Residential initiative for the renewal of the historic center.
Future urban investments in the rehabilitation area of the City Hall and municipal administration buildings (approximate cost ATS 120 million).
Development of a cultural axis (Eisernes Haus, Mariahilferplatz/Cultural Center Minoritenzentrum, Schlossberg tunnel, University Campus, greenhouses/Botanical Gardens).
Schlossberg:
Rehabilitation and architectural revitalisation: Clock Tower with forecourt, bell tower, casemates, Chinese pavilion, tunnel, securing of paths (approximate costs ATS 45 million), Cerrini-Schlössl and Starke-Häuschen (approximate costs ATS 11 million), paths and parks (approximate costs ATS 20 million).

4 | Management

a | The historic center in the zone proposed for inclusion on the World Heritage List includes 450 historic monuments.
The major part is privately owned by families who have been living here for generations and whose awareness of traditional values ensures the perfect preservation of these buildings. Moreover, full legal protection is also guaranteed (see 4b).
The latter also extends to numerous buildings owned by the Republic of Austria, the province of Styria and the city of Graz, as well as by other corporations under public law and the legally recognised churches.

b | The scheme for the preservation of the historic center of Graz encompasses a number of overlapping levels:

1 | Zur Erhaltung der Altstadt und zur Aktivierung ihrer vielfältigen urbanen Funktionen wurde 1980 das „Grazer Altstadterhaltungsgesetz (GAEG)" geschaffen.
Das Erscheinungsbild des historischen Zentrums ist nach diesem Gesetz insgesamt geschützt. Das GAEG schützt Baudenkmäler ebenso wie Straßen- und Platzräume, Kleindenkmäler, Freiräume etc.
2 | Eine weitere Schutzebene ist durch das Denkmalschutzgesetz von 1923 (DMSG) gegeben. Es konzentriert sich auf die herausragenden Baudenkmäler (in der Zone derzeit 125 von 450 Bauwerken). Der Denkmalschutz umfasst über das Erscheinungsbild (nach dem GAEG) hinaus die volle Dimension der Substanz und überlieferten Erscheinung.
3 | Bauordnung: Alle Baubewilligungen im historischen Zentrum müssen sich in ihren Entscheidungen nach dem GAEG bzw. dem DMSG orientieren.
4 | Ein Parkerhaltungs- und -pflegegesetz ist in Vorbereitung.

c | Der flächendeckende Schutz des historischen Zentrums von Graz bedeutet, dass jede Veränderung, die die historische Substanz, die überlieferte Erscheinung und künstlerische Wirkung betrifft, des Einvernehmens bzw. der Genehmigung nach dem GAEG und dem DMSG bedarf.

d, e | Folgende Institutionen (mit erfahrenen Fachexperten – Architekten, KunsthistorikerInnen, Stadtplaner, Archäologen) managen u. a. die Erhaltung der Grazer Altstadt:
Altstadterhaltungskommission,
Paulustorgasse 4, A-8010 Graz
Amt für Stadtentwicklung und Stadterhaltung,
Europaplatz 20, A-8020 Graz
Bundesdenkmalamt,
Schubertstraße 73, A-8010 Graz

f | In Graz ist eine – gemessen an Größe und Einwohnerzahl – unverhältnismäßig breite und produktive Kulturszene zu finden. Dies verdankt die Stadt ihren Hochschulen, ihrer multiethnisch und multikonfessionell geprägten Einwohnerschaft und vor allem einer großen Zahl an Einrichtungen für Kulturproduktionen und -veranstaltungen: Das Internationale Städteforum Graz ist ein Dokumentations- und Informationszentrum, widmet sich dem

1 | In order to ensure the preservation of the historic center and the activation of its diverse urban functions the "Grazer Altstadterhaltungsgesetz (GAEG)" (Graz Historic Center Conservation Act) was introduced in 1980 (see enclosure). This act protects the appearance of the historic center in its entirety. The GAEG protects architectural monuments as well as streets and squares, small monuments, open spaces, etc.
2 | Another protective level is provided by the Monument Protection Act of 1923 (Denkmalschutzgesetz/DMSG). It concentrates on outstanding historic monuments and goes beyond the outward appearance (under GAEG) to include the whole dimension of the building material and the traditional appearance.
3 | Building code: All building permits in the historic center are subject to provisions of the GAEG and DMSG.
4 | An act dealing with the preservation and care of parks is being prepared.

c | The comprehensive protection of the historic center of Graz means that any alteration involving the historic substance, the traditional appearance and the artistic effect is subject to agreement and approval according to the GAEG and DMSG.

d, e | The following institutions are in charge of the preservation of the historic center of Graz (assisted by specialists, such as architects, art historians, city planners, archeologists).
Historic Center Conservation Commission,
Paulustorgasse 4, A-8010 Graz
Municipal Planning and Design Office,
Europaplatz 20, A-8020 Graz
Federal Office of Historical Monuments,
Schubertstraße 73, A-8010 Graz

f | For a city of its size and number of inhabitants, Graz boasts a disproportionately large and productive cultural scene. This is due to its universities, its multi-ethnic and multidenominational population and above all to the large number of institutions organising cultural productions and events: Internationales Städteforum (International Town Forum Graz) is a documentation and information center dedicated to the exchange of experience

Erfahrungsaustausch (Kongresse, Vorträge, Ausstellungen etc.) in Bezug auf Erhaltung, Restaurierung und Adaptierung historisch wertvoller Stadt- und Ortszentren. Darüber hinaus ist im Städteforum das Archiv zu den jährlich ausgeschriebenen „Europa Nostra"-Wettbewerben eingerichtet.

Der „steirische herbst" zählt zu den wichtigsten internationalen Festivals der Gegenwartskunst. Von seinem seit 1966 jährlich stattfindenden vielspartigen Programm gehen Impulse aus, die das internationale Kunstgeschehen maßgeblich beeinflussen.

Die alle zwei Jahre veranstalteten Trigon-Ausstellungen stellten seit 1963 zeitgenössische Kunstwerke aus Slowenien, Kroatien, Italien, Österreich und Ungarn einander gegenüber.

Vom Forum Stadtpark gehen seit Jahrzehnten Impulse für die Avantgarde der Literatur, der Bildenden Künste und der Fotografie aus, dokumentiert etwa in der renommierten Literaturzeitschrift „manuskripte" oder in der internationalen Fotozeitschrift „Camera austria".

Das Kulturhaus der Stadt Graz ist der Ort für die Präsentation der internationalen Kunst des 20. Jahrhunderts.

Das junge Haus der Architektur hat sich in kürzester Zeit weltweiten Ruf als Diskussionsforum neuester Architekturströmungen geschaffen („Grazer Schule der Architektur").

Seit 1985 besteht die styriarte, ein hochkarätiges Festival für klassische Musik.

Ein Opernhaus und ein Schauspielhaus, die Vereinigten Bühnen, mit ständigem Ensemble, Orchester, Chor und Ballett bieten ein reiches und vielfältiges Theaterangebot.

Das Landesmuseum Joanneum (zweitgrößtes Museum Österreichs, 1811) mit seinen 16 Abteilungen trägt den Preis des Europarates für das „Europäische Museum des Jahres 1984". Zu ihm gehören das Barockjuwel Schloss Eggenberg ebenso wie das Landeszeughaus, die weltgrößte Sammlung von Waffen aus der Zeit der Türkenkriege.

Das Grazer Stadtmuseum ist eine Einrichtung zur Aufarbeitung und Präsentation der Geschichte der Stadt.

Weitere aktuelle Promotionsaktivitäten:

Imagesteigerung und Förderung des Standortes Graz-Altstadt durch Förderung von Eventveranstaltungen wie zum Beispiel La Strada, Graz erzählt, AIMS, Classic in the City, Advent der Regionen, styriate, Jazz-Sommer, CNN – Cultural City Network, Kunst- und Kulturvermittlung (Kosten ca. 15 Millionen/Jahr).

(congresses, lectures, exhibitions, etc.) regarding the preservation, restoration and adaptation of historically valuable city and village centers. Moreover, the Städteforum contains the archives for the annual "Europa Nostra" competitions.

"steirischer herbst" counts as one of the most important international festivals of contemporary art. Held annually since 1966, its extensive multisection programme creates waves of significant impact on the international scene.

Since 1963, the Trigon exhibitions have been organised every two years, presenting contemporary works of art from Slovenia, Croatia, Italy, Austria and Hungary.

For several decades, Forum Stadtpark has stimulated the avantgarde of literature, visual arts and photography, documented by the renowned literary periodical "manuskripte" and by the international photography journal "Camera austria".

International 20th-century art is exhibited in the Kulturhaus der Stadt Graz (Cultural Center of the City of Graz). The newly established Haus der Architektur (Center for Architecture) has quickly gained world-wide renown as a forum for discussion of the latest architectural trends ("Grazer Schule der Architektur", Graz School of Architecture).

"styriarte", a highly respected festival for classical music, was founded in 1985.

An opera house and a theatre, the Vereinigten Bühnen (Theatre Association), with their permanent companies, orchestra, choir and ballet offer a rich and varied spectrum of drama.

The Provincial Museum Joanneum (oldest Austrian regional museum, founded in 1811) with 16 sections won the European Council "European Museum of the year 1984" award. It includes the Baroque gem of the Eggenberg Palace as well as the Styrian armoury, the largest collection in the world of weapons from the time of the Turkish wars.

The City Museum of Graz is an institution that studies and presents the history of the city.

Other current promotional activities:

Image boosting and promotion of the historic center of Graz by subsidised events such as La Strada, Graz erzählt (Graz tells a story), AIMS, Classic in the City, Advent of the Regions, styriarte, Jazz Summer, CNN – Cultural City Network, Kunst- und Kulturvermittlung (approximate cost ATS 15 million per year).

g | Zur Erhaltung, Konservierung und Restaurierung stehen aus den Mitteln des Altstadterhaltungsfonds jährlich 4,4 Millionen Schilling zur Verfügung. Dazu kommen Mittel des Landes Steiermark aus dem Revitalisierungsfonds in der Höhe von 3,175 Millionen Schilling jährlich sowie die Subventionen des Bundesdenkmalamtes und des Bundesministeriums für Unterricht und kulturelle Angelegenheiten nach dem Denkmalschutzgesetz.
Einen wesentlichen Teil der Erhaltungsmaßnahmen tragen nach wie vor die Eigentümer der Bauwerke.
Mit den zusätzlichen, in Kapitel 3 e angeführten finanziellen Mitteln können die zur Verfügung stehenden Ressourcen als ausreichend angesehen werden.

h | Für die Konservierung und das Management in den genannten Einrichtungen mit Leitungskompetenzen stehen Fachexperten mit Studienrichtungen Kunstgeschichte, Architektur, Archäologie, Restaurierung, Stadtplanung und Wirtschaft zur Verfügung. Für spezielles Training im Bereich Konservierung und Restaurierung sind im Bundesdenkmalamt zwei zentrale Restaurierwerkstätten (für Baudenkmalpflege und Kunstdenkmäler) eingerichtet, wo u. a. auch ICCROM Kurse stattfinden.

i, j, k | Die Altstadt von Graz ist nicht musealisiert, sie ist im Gegenteil bevorzugtes Zentrum für kulturelles Leben (siehe 4 f.). Von der Stadtverwaltung wird dabei aber besonderes Augenmerk auf die Gegebenheiten eines „sanften Tourismus" gelegt.

5 | Faktoren, die sich auf das Kulturgut auswirken

a | Störende Eingriffe in die historische Bausubstanz sind durch die rechtlichen Vorgaben (siehe Pkt. 4 b) ausgeschlossen.
Durch die Grundrissstruktur der Stadt, die umgebende Erweiterung des 19. Jahrhunderts und den geschützten ausgedehnten Grüngürtel um die Altstadt ist das historische Zentrum von Graz in Bezug auf wirtschaftlichen Entwicklungsdruck und Umweltprobleme maximal geschützt. Durch nach wie vor vorhandene ausgewogene soziale Strukturen existiert kein großer Veränderungsdruck im Wohnbereich. Gegen negative Einflüsse durch den Fremdenverkehr ist Vorsorge getroffen.

b | Gegen Umweltbelastungen wurden folgende aktuelle Maßnahmen zur Reduzierung der Umweltbelastungen gesetzt: Ge-

g | For purposes of preservation, conservation and restoration, the Historic Center Conservation Fund has an annual sum of ATS 4.4 million at its disposal. Additional resources include ATS 3.175 million provided annually by the renewal fund of the province of Styria, as well as the aid granted by the Federal Office of Historic Monuments and the Federal Ministry of Education and Cultural Affairs under the Monument Protection Act.
A major part of the conservation efforts is still being financed by the owners of the buildings themselves.
Together with the additional financial means listed in item 3e, the available resources can be considered sufficient.

h | Experts in the fields of art history, architecture, archeology, restoration, city planning and economy are in charge of conservation and management in the agencies with the management authority mentioned above. Two central restoration workshops (for the care of architectural and artistic monuments) in the Federal Office of Historic Monuments provide special training in the fields of conservation and restoration and arrange ICCROM courses.

i, j, k | The historic center of Graz is not a museum showpiece but a popular center for cultural life (see 4f). However, the municipal administration is according special priority to the creation of an infrastructure for "environmentally sensitive tourism".

5 | Factors Affecting the Property

a | Legal provisions exclude undesirable encroachment factors with regard to the historic building material (see 4b).
The historic center of Graz enjoys maximum protection against development pressures and environmental pressures due to the structure of its ground plan, the expansion zones of the 19th century that surround it, and the extensive protected green belt. Thanks to the balanced social structure there is little pressure for change in the residental area. Precautions have been taken against negative tourism pressure.

b | The following measures have been taken for the reduction of environmental pressures: general traffic limitations, creation of

nerelle Verkehrsbeschränkungen, Fußgängerzonen, Temporeduzierung des öffentlichen Verkehrs (Aktionen „Platz für Menschen", „Tempo 30/50") und restriktive Kurzparkzonenüberwachung.

c | Der Fluss Mur wurde in der Vergangenheit so reguliert, dass es zu keinen gefährlichen Überschwemmungen kommen kann.

d | Eine engagierte Stadtpolitik bemüht sich, den Tourismus in ausgewogenen Bahnen zu halten.

e | Die Einwohnerzahl hat sich in jüngster Zeit nicht verändert; sie beträgt in der Kernzone 5.863 Personen, in der Pufferzone 4.603.

6 | Überwachung

a–c | Eine ständige Kontrolle des Erhaltungszustandes ist gegeben: durch die Grazer Altstadterhaltungskommission, die Baubehörde, Überwachung durch das Bundesdenkmalamt, Landeskonservatorat Steiermark, wobei die Stadt Graz für das Stadtbild insgesamt, das Bundesdenkmalamt für die Überwachung der denkmalgeschützten Objekte zuständig ist.
In den letzten Jahren wurden an über 50 % der 450 Baudenkmale und an nahezu allen der unter Denkmalschutz stehenden Objekten Konservierungs- und Restaurierungsmaßnahmen zur Erhaltung der Substanz, der überlieferten Erscheinung und der künstlerischen Wirkung vorgenommen. Sanierungsmaßnahmen an weiteren Bauten sind vorbereitet bzw. eingeleitet. Die kontinuierliche Pflege ist damit gesichert.
Die Altstadterhaltungskommission bearbeitet jährlich zwischen 600–700 Interventionen.

EVALUIERUNG

Die von der Stadt Graz in Zusammenarbeit mit dem Bundesdenkmalamt über das Bundesministerium für Unterricht und Kunst eingereichte Dokumentation (Einreichung Mai 1998) wurde im Auftrag der UNESCO von einem Experten der ICOMOS (Internationaler Rat für Denkmalpflege) evaluiert. Bei einem zweitägigen Stadtbesuch im Jänner 1999 und die Besichtigung der Altstadt und der gründerzeitlichen Pufferzonen (II., III.

pedestrian zones, speed reduction of public transport (campaigns "Platz für Menschen" (Room for people), "Speed 30/50" and a restrictive supervision of limited parking zones.

c | Regulation of the river Mur carried out in the past prevents dangerous flooding.

d | Tourism is being kept within reasonable limits through an active urban policy.

e | The number of inhabitants has not changed recently; it stands at 5,863 within the core zone and 4,603 in the buffer zone.

6 | **Monitoring**

a–c | The state of conservation is monitored constantly: by the Graz Historic Center Conservation Commission, the building authority, the Federal Office of Historic Monuments, the Styrian Conservation Office. The Municipality of Graz is responsible for the townscape generally, the Federal Office of Historic Monuments for the monitoring of the protected objects. In recent years, conservation and restoration works were carried out on more than 50 per cent of the 450 historic monuments and on almost all of the protected objects, with the purpose of preserving their fabric, traditional appearance and artistic effect. Rehabilitation measures concerning further structures are being prepared or have already been launched. This ensures care of the monuments on a permanent basis.
The Historic Center Conservation Commission handles about 600-700 interventions per year.

EVALUATION

The documentation, submitted from the city of Graz in collaboration with the Federal Monument Office and via the Federal Ministry for Education and Art (submission made in May 1998), was evaluated on behalf of UNESCO by an expert from ICOMOS (International Council of Monuments and Sites). In January 1999, during a two-day visit to the old town and the boom-time buffer zones (Area II, III), the ICOMOS expert checked the documenta-

Bezirk) überprüfte der ICOMOS Fachmann die Dokumentation nach den entsprechenden Kriterien der UNESCO-Konvention. Das abschließende Evaluierungsgutachen wurde von einem ICOMOS Fachgremium im April 1999 bestätigt und führte zu einer positiven Empfehlung des Internationalen Rates für Denkmalpflege (ICOMOS) an das Büro des World Heritage Comitees der UNESCO in Paris zur Aufnahme in die Welterbeliste.

DIE ERNENNUNG

In einer Sitzung gab dieses Büro im Juli 1999 an das UNESCO-World Heritage Comitee folgende Empfehlung ab:
„Das Büro empfahl dem Komitee, diese Stätte in die Liste der Weltkulturerbestätten auf Basis der Kriterien (II) und (IV) aufzunehmen.
Kriterium (II): Das Altstadtzentrum der Stadt Graz reflektiert künstlerische und architektonische Bewegungen, die vom germanischen Raum, dem Balkan und dem Mittelmeerraum ausgegangen sind, da die Stadt über Jahrhunderte einen Kreuzungspunkt zwischen diesen Regionen darstellte. Die größten Künstler und Architekten dieser unterschiedlichen Gebiete schufen hier eindrucksvolle Arbeiten und eine brillante Synthese.
Kriterium (IV): Der städtische Komplex des Altstadtzentrums von Graz ist ein außergewöhnliches Beispiel für die harmonische Integration architektonischer Stilarten verschiedener Perioden. Jedes Zeitalter ist durch charakteristische Bauten, die oft wahre Meisterstücke sind, vertreten. Die städtische Physiognomie erzählt die Geschichte der historischen Entwicklung der Stadt wahrheitsgetreu."

Die Ernennung zum Weltkulturerbe Graz Altstadt erfolgte am 1. 12. 1999 in Marrakesch.

tion according to the corresponding criteria of the UNESCO convention. The resulting evaluation of the expert's report was confirmed by an ICOMOS expert committee in April 1999, and led to the International Council of Monuments and Sites' positive recommendation that the UNESCO Bureau of the World Heritage Committee in Paris should include the Historic Center of Graz on the World Heritage List.

LISTING

In a meeting in July 1999, this bureau made the following recommendation to the UNESCO World Heritage Committee:
"The Bureau recommended that the Committee include this site on the World Heritage List on the basis of the cultural criteria (II) and (IV).
Criterion (II): The historic center of the city of Graz reflects artistic and architectural movements originating from the Germanic region, the Balkans, and the Mediterranean, for which it served as a crossroads for centuries. The greatest architects and artists of these various regions expressed themselves forcefully here and so created a brilliant synthesis.
Criterion (IV): The urban complex forming the historic center of the city of Graz is an exceptional example of a harmonious integration of architectural styles from successive periods. Each age is represented by typical buildings, which are often masterpieces. The urban physiognomy faithfully tells the story of its historic development."

The inscription of Graz Historic Center was carried out on December 1, 1999 in Marrakech.

Appendix

Anhang VI

Liste der Weltkulturerbestätten

ALBANIA
1992 Butrint

ALGERIA
1980 Al Qal'a of Beni Hammad
1982 Tassili n'Ajjer
1982 M'Zab Valley
1982 Djémila
1982 Tipasa
1982 Timgad
1992 Kasbah of Algiers

ARGENTINA
1981 Los Glaciares
1984 Iguazu National Park
1999 Cueva de las Manos, Río Pinturas
1999 Península Valdés

ARGENTINA AND BRAZIL
1984 Jesuit Missions of the Guaranis
San Ignacio Mini, Santa Ana, Nuestra Señora de Loreto and Santa Maria Mayor (Argentina), Ruins of Sao Miguel das Missoes (Brazil)

ARMENIA
1996 Monastery of Haghpat

AUSTRALIA
1981 Great Barrier Reef
1981 Kakadu National Park
1981 Willandra Lakes Region
1982 Tasmanian Wilderness
1982 Lord Howe Island Group
1987 Uluru-Kata Tjuta National Park
1987 Central Eastern Rainforest Reserves (Australia)
1988 Wet Tropics of Queensland
1991 Shark Bay, Western Australia
1992 Fraser Island
1994 Australian Fossil Mammal Sites (Riversleigh/Naracoorte)
1997 Heard and McDonald Islands
1997 Macquarie Island

AUSTRIA
1996 Historic Centre of the City of Salzburg
1996 Palace and Gardens of Schönbrunn
1997 Hallstatt-Dachstein Salzkammergut Cultural Landscape
1998 Semmering Railway
1999 City of Graz – Historic Centre

BANGLADESH
1985 Historic Mosque City of Bagerhat
1985 Ruins of the Buddhist Vihara at Paharpur
1997 The Sundarbans

BELARUS/POLAND
1992 Belovezhskaya Pushcha/Bialowieza Forest

BELGIUM
1998 Flemish Béguinages
1998 The Four Lifts on the Canal du Centre and their Environs, La Louvière and Le Roeulx (Hainault)
1998 Grand-Place, Brussels
1999 Belfries of Flanders and Wallonia

BELIZE
1996 Belize Barrier Reef Reserve System

BENIN
1985 Royal Palaces of Abomey

BOLIVIA
1987 City of Potosi
1990 Jesuit Missions of the Chiquitos
1991 Historic City of Sucre
1998 El Fuerte de Samaipata

BRAZIL
1980 Historic Town of Ouro Preto
1982 Historic Centre of the Town of Olinda
1985 Historic Centre of Salvador de Bahia
1985 Sanctuary of Bom Jesus do Congonhas
1986 Iguacu National Park
1987 Brasilia
1991 Serra da Capivara National Park
1997 The Historic Centre of São Luis
1999 Historic Centre of the Town of Diamantina
1999 Discovery Coast Atlantic Forest Reserves
1999 Atlantic Forest Southeast Reserves

BULGARIA
1979 Boyana Church
1979 Madara Rider
1979 Rock-hewn Churches of Ivanovo
1979 Thracian tomb of Kazanlak
1983 Ancient City of Nessebar
1983 Srebarna Nature Reserve
1983 Pirin National Park

1983 Rila Monastery
1985 Thracian tomb of Sveshtari

CAMBODIA
1992 Angkor

CAMEROON
1987 Dja Faunal Reserve

CANADA
1978 L'Anse aux Meadows National Historic Park
1978 Nahanni National Park
1979 Dinosaur Provincial Park
1981 Anthony Island
1981 Head-Smashed-In Buffalo Jump Complex
1983 Wood Buffalo National Park
1984 Canadian Rocky Mountain Parks*
1985 Quebec (Historic Area)
1987 Gros Morne National Park
1995 Lunenburg Old Town
1999 Miguasha Park
*The Burgess Shale Site, previously inscribed on the WHL, is part of the Canadian Rocky Mountain Parks.

CANADA AND THE UNITED STATES OF AMERICA
1979 Tatshenshini-Alsek/Kluane National Park/Wrangell-St. Elias National Park and Reserve and Glacier Bay National Park
1995 Waterton Glacier International Peace Park

CENTRAL AFRICAN REPUBLIC
1988 Manovo-Gounda St. Floris National Park

CHILE
1995 Rapa Nui National Park

CHINA
1987 The Great Wall
1987 Mount Taishan
1987 Imperial Palace of the Ming and Qing Dynasties
1987 Mogao Caves
1987 Mausoleum of the First Qin Emporer
1987 Peking Man Site at Zhoukoudian
1990 Mount Huangshan
1992 Jiuzhaigou Valley Scenic and Historic Interest Area
1992 Huanglong Scenic and Historic Interest Area
1992 Wulingyuan Scenic and Historic Interest Area
1994 The Mountain Resort and its Outlying Temples, Chengde
1994 Temple and Cemetery of Confucius, and the Kong Family Mansion in Qufu
1994 Ancient Building Complex in the Wudang Mountains
1994 Potala Palace, Lhasa
1996 Lushan National Park
1996 Mount Emei and Leshan Giant Buddha
1997 Old Town of Lijiang
1997 Ancient City of Ping Yao
1997 Classical Gardens of Suzhou
1998 Summer Palace, an Imperial Garden in Beijing
1998 Temple of Heaven – an Imperial Sacrificial Altar in Beijing
1999 Mount Wuyi
1999 Dazu Rock Carvings

COLOMBIA
1984 Port, Fortresses and Group of Monuments, Cartagena
1994 Los Katios National Park
1995 Historic Centre of Santa Cruz de Mompox
1995 National Archaeological Park of Tierradentro
1995 San Agustín Archaeological Park

COSTA RICA
1997 Cocos Island National Park
1999 Area de Conservación Guanacaste

COSTA RICA/PANAMA
1983 Talamanca Range-La Amistad Reserves/ La Amistad National Park

COTE D'IVOIRE
1982 Taï National Park
1983 Comoé National Park

CROATIA
1979 Old City of Dubrovnik
1979 Historic Complex of Split with the Palace of Diocletian
1979 Plitvice Lakes National Park
1997 Episcopal Complex of the Euphrasian Basilica in the Historic Centre of Porec
1997 Historic City of Trogir

CUBA
1982 Old Havana and its Fortifications
1988 Trinidad and the Valley de los Ingenios
1997 San Pedro de la Roca Castle, Santiago de Cuba
1999 Desembarco del Granma National Park
1999 Viñales Valley

VI

CYPRUS
1980 Paphos
1985 Painted Churches in the Troodos Region
1998 Choirokoitia

CZECH REPUBLIC
1992 Historic Centre of Prague
1992 Historic Centre of Cesky Krumlov
1992 Historic Centre of Telc
1994 Pilgrimage Church of St. John of Nepomuk at Zelena Hora
1995 Kutná Hora Historical Town Centre with the Church of Saint Barbara and the Cathedral of our Lady at Sedlec
1996 Lednice-Valtice Cultural Landscape
1998 Holasŏvice Historical Village Reservation
1998 Gardens and Castle at Kromeríz
1999 Litomyšl Castle

DEMOCRATIC REPUBLIC OF THE CONGO
1979 Virunga National Park
1980 Kahuzi-Biega National Park
1980 Garamba National Park
1984 Salonga National Park
1996 Okapi Wildlife Reserve

DENMARK
1994 Jellings Mounds, Runic Stones and Church
1995 Roskilde Cathedral

DOMINICA
1997 Morne Trois Pitons National Park

DOMINICAN REPUBLIC
1990 Colonial City of Santo Domingo

ECUADOR
1978 Galapagos Islands
1978 City of Quito
1983 Sangay National Park
1999 Historic Centre of Santa Ana de los Rios de Cuenca

EGYPT
1979 Memphis and its Necropolis – the Pyramid Fields from Giza to Dahshur
1979 Ancient Thebes with its Necropolis
1979 Nubian Monuments from Abu Simbel to Philae
1979 Islamic Cairo
1979 Abu Mena

EL SALVADOR
1993 Joya de Ceren Archaeological Site

ESTONIA
1997 The Historic Centre (Old Town) of Tallinn

ETHIOPIA
1978 Rock-hewn Churches, Lalibela
1978 Simen National Park
1979 Fasil Ghebbi, Gondar Region
1980 Aksum
1980 Lower Valley of the Awash
1980 Lower Valley of the Omo
1980 Tiya

FINLAND
1991 Old Rauma
1991 Fortress of Suomenlinna
1994 Petäjävesi Old Church
1996 Verla Groundwood and Board Mill
1999 Bronze Age Burial Site of Sammallahdenmäki

FORMER YUGOSLAV REP. OF MACEDONIA
1979 Ohrid Region, including its cultural and historic aspects, and its natural environment

FRANCE
1979 Mont-Saint-Michel and its Bay
1979 Chartres Cathedral
1979 Palace and Park of Versailles
1979 Vézelay, Church and Hill
1979 Decorated Grottoes of the Vézère Valley
1981 Palace and Park of Fontainebleau
1981 Chateau and Estate of Chambord
1981 Amiens Cathedral
1981 Roman Theatre and its Surroundings and the "Triumphal Arch" of Orange
1981 Roman and Romanesque Monuments of Arles
1981 Cistercian Abbey of Fontenay
1982 Royal Saltworks of Arc-et-Senans
1983 Place Stanislas, Place de la Carrière and Place d'Alliance in Nancy
1983 Church of Saint-Savin sur Gartempe
1983 Cape Girolata, Cape Porto, Scandola Natural Reserve and the Piana Calanches in Corsica
1985 Pont du Gard (Roman Aqueduct)
1988 Strasbourg-Grande îsle

1991 Paris, Banks of the Seine
1991 Cathedral of Notre-Dame, Former Abbey of Saint-Remi and Palace of Tau, Reims
1992 Bourges Cathedral
1995 Historic Centre of Avignon
1996 Canal du Midi
1997 Historic Fortified City of Carcassonne
1998 Routes of Santiago de Compostela in France
1998 Historic Site of Lyons
1999 Jurisdiction of Saint-Emilion

FRANCE/SPAIN
1997 Pyrénées - Mount Perdu

GEORGIA
1994 City-Museum Reserve of Mtskheta
1994 Bagrati Cathedral and Gelati Monastery
1996 Upper Svaneti

GERMANY
1978 Aachen Cathedral
1981 Speyer Cathedral
1981 Würzburg Residence, with the Court Gardens and Residence Square
1983 Pilgrimage Church of Wies
1984 The Castles of Augustusburg and Falkenlust at Brühl
1985 St. Mary's Cathedral and St. Michael's Church at Hildesheim
1986 Roman Monuments, Cathedral and Liebfrauen-Church in Trier
1987 Hanseatic City of Lübeck
1990 Palaces and Parks of Potsdam and Berlin
1991 Abbey and Altenmünster of Lorsch
1992 Mines of Rammelsberg and Historic Town of Goslar
1993 Town of Bamberg
1993 Maulbronn Monastery Complex
1994 Collegiate Church, Castle, and old Town of Quedlinburg
1994 Völklingen Ironworks
1995 Messel Pit Fossil site
1996 Cologne Cathedral
1996 Bauhaus and its sites in Weimar and Dessau
1996 Luther Memorials in Eisleben and Wittenberg
1998 Classical Weimar
1999 Museumsinsel (Museum Island), Berlin
1999 Wartburg Castle

GHANA
1979 Forts and Castles, Volta Greater Accra, Central and Western Regions

1980 Ashanti Traditional Buildings

GREECE
1986 Temple of Apollo Epicurius at Bassae
1987 Archaeological Site of Delphi
1987 Acropolis, Athens
1988 Mount Athos
1988 Meteora
1988 Paleochristian and Byzantine Monuments of Thessalonika
1988 Archaeological Site of Epidaurus
1988 Medieval City of Rhodes
1989 Mystras
1989 Archaeological Site of Olympia
1990 Delos
1990 Monasteries of Daphni, Hossios Luckas and Nea Moni of Chios
1992 Pythagoreion and Heraion of Samos
1996 Archaeological Site of Vergina
1999 Archaeological Sites of Mycenae and Tiryns
1999 Historic Centre (Chorá) with the Monastery of Saint John "the Theologian" and the Cave of the Apocalypse on the Island of Pátmos

GUATEMALA
1979 Tikal National Park
1979 Antigua Guatemala
1981 Archaeological Park and Ruins of Quirigua

GUINEA AND COTE D'IVOIRE
1981 Mount Nimba Strict Nature Reserve

HAITI
1982 National History Park – Citadel, Sans-Souci, Ramiers

HOLY SEE
1984 Vatican City

HONDURAS
1980 Maya Site of Copan
1982 Rio Platano Biosphere Reserve

HUNGARY
1987 Budapest, the Banks of the Danube and the Buda Castle Quarter
1987 Hollokö
1996 Millenary Benedictine Monastery of Pannonhalma and its Natural Environment
1999 Hortobágy National Park

VI

HUNGARY AND SLOVAKIA
1995 Caves of the Aggtelek and Slovak Karst

INDIA
1983 Ajanta Caves
1983 Ellora Caves
1983 Agra Fort
1983 Taj Mahal
1984 Sun Temple, Konarak
1985 Group of Monuments at Mahabalipuram
1985 Kaziranga National Park
1985 Manas Wildlife Sanctuary
1985 Keoladeo National Park
1986 Churches and Convents of Goa
1986 Khajuraho Group of Monuments
1986 Group of Monuments at Hampi
1986 Fatehpur Sikri
1987 Group of Monuments at Pattadakal
1987 Elephanta Caves
1987 Brihadisvara Temple, Thanjavur
1987 Sundarbans National Park
1988 Nanda Devi National Park
1989 Buddhist Monuments at Sanchi
1993 Humayun's Tomb, Delhi
1993 Qutb Minar and its Monuments, Delhi
1999 Darjeeling Himalayan Railway

INDONESIA
1991 Borobudur Temple Compounds
1991 Ujung Kulon National Park
1991 Komodo National Park
1991 Prambanan Temple Compounds
1996 Sangiran Early Man Site
1999 Lorentz National Park

IRAN
1979 Tchogha Zanbil
1979 Persepolis
1979 Meidan Emam, Esfahan

IRAQ
1985 Hatra

IRELAND
1993 Archaeological Ensemble of the Bend of the Boyne
1996 Skellig Michael

ITALY
1979 Rock Drawings in Valcamonica
1980 The Church and Dominican Convent of Santa Maria delle Grazie with "The Last Supper" by Leonardo da Vinci
1982 Historic Centre of Florence
1987 Venice and its Lagoon
1987 Piazza del Duomo, Pisa
1990 Historic Centre of San Gimignano
1993 I Sassi di Matera
1994 City of Vicenza and the Palladian Villas of the Veneto
1995 Historic Centre of Siena
1995 Historic Centre of Naples
1995 Crespi d'Adda
1995 Ferrara, City of the Renaissance and its Po Delta
1996 Castel del Monte
1996 The trulli of Alberobello
1996 Early Christian Monuments of Ravenna
1996 Historic Centre of the City of Pienza
1997 18th-Century Royal Palace at Caserta with the Park, the Aqueduct of Vanvitelli and the San Leucio Complex
1997 Residences of the Royal House of Savoy
1997 Botanical Garden (Orto Botanico), Padua
1997 Portovenere, Cinque Terre, and the Islands (Palmaria, Tino and Tinetto)
1997 Cathedral, Torre Civica and Piazza Grande, Modena
1997 Archaeological Areas of Pompei, Herculaneum, and Torre Annunziata
1997 Costiera Amalfitana
1997 Archaeological Area of Agrigento
1997 Villa Romana del Casale
1997 Su Nuraxi di Barumini
1998 Cilento and Vallo di Diano National Park with the Archeological sites of Paestum and Velia, and the Certosa di Padula
1998 Historic Centre of Urbino
1998 Archaeological Area and the Patriarchal Basilica of Aquileia
1999 Villa Adriana

ITALY/HOLY SEE
1980 Historic centre of Rome, the Properties of the Holy See in that City Enjoying Extraterritorial Rights, and San Paolo Fuori le Mura

JAPAN
1993 Buddhist Monuments in the Horyu-ji Area
1993 Himeji-jo
1993 Yakushima
1993 Shirakami-Sanchi
1994 Historic Monuments of Ancient Kyoto (Kyoto, Uji and Otsu Cities)

1995 Historic Villages of Shirakawa-go and Gokayama
1996 Hiroshima Peace Memorial (Genbaku Dome)
1996 Itsukushima Shinto Shrine
1998 Historic Monuments of Ancient Nara
1999 Shrines and Temples of Nikko

JERUSALEM
1981 Old City of Jerusalem and its Walls (site proposed by Jordan)

JORDAN
1985 Petra
1985 Quseir Amra

KENYA
1997 Mount Kenya National Park/Natural Forest
1997 Sibiloi/Central Island National Parks

LAO PEOPLE'S DEMOCRATIC REPUBLIC
1995 Town of Luang Prabang

LATVIA
1997 Historic Centre of Riga

LEBANON
1984 Anjar
1984 Baalbek
1984 Byblos
1984 Tyre
1998 Ouadi Qadisha (the Holy Valley) and the Forest of the Cedars of God (Horsh Arz el-Rab)

LIBYAN ARAB JAMAHIRIYA
1982 Archaeological Site of Leptis Magna
1982 Archaeological Site of Sabratha
1982 Archaeological Site of Cyrene
1985 Rock-art Sites of Tadrart Acacus
1988 Old Town of Ghadames

LITHUANIA
1994 Vilnius Historic Centre

LUXEMBOURG
1994 City of Luxemburg its Old Quarters and Fortifications

MADAGASCAR
1990 Tsingy de Bemaraha Strict Nature Reserve

MALAWI
1984 Lake Malawi National Park

MALI
1988 Old Towns of Djenné
1988 Timbuktu
1989 Cliff of Bandiagara (Land of the Dogons)

MALTA
1980 Hal Saflieni Hypogeum
1980 City of Valetta
1980 Megalithic Temples of Malta

MAURITANIA
1989 Banc d'Arguin National Park
1996 Ancient ksour of Ouadane, Chinguetti, Tichitt and Oualata

MEXICO
1987 Sian Ka'an
1987 Pre-Hispanic City and National Park of Palenque
1987 Historic Centre of Mexico City and Xochimilco
1987 Pre-Hispanic City of Teotihuacan
1987 Historic Centre of Oaxaca and Archaeological Site of Monte Alban
1987 Historic Centre of Puebla
1988 Historic Town of Guanajuato and Adjacent Mines
1988 Pre-Hispanic City of Chichen-Itza
1991 Historic Centre of Morelia
1992 El Tajin, Pre-Hispanic City
1993 Whale Sanctuary of El Vizcaino
1993 Historic Centre of Zacatecas
1993 Rock Paintings of the Sierra de San Francisco
1994 Earliest 16th-Century Monasteries on the Slopes of Popocatepetl
1996 Prehispanic Town of Uxmal
1996 Historic Monuments Zone of Querétaro
1997 Hospicio Cabanas, Guadalajara
1998 Historic Monuments Zone of Tlacotalpan
1998 Archeological zone of Paquimé, Casas Grandes
1999 Historic Fortified Town of Campeche
1999 Archaeological Monuments Zone of Xochicalco

MOROCCO
1981 Medina of Fez
1985 Medina of Marrakesh
1987 Ksar of Aït-Ben-Haddou
1996 Historic City of Meknes
1997 Archaeological Site of Volubilis

VI

1997 The Medina of Tétouan (formerly known as Titawin)

MOZAMBIQUE
1991 Island of Mozambique

NEPAL
1979 Sagarmatha National Park
1979 Kathmandu Valley
1984 Royal Chitwan National Park
1997 Lumbini, the Birthplace of the Lord Buddha

NETHERLANDS
1995 Schokland and Surroundings
1996 Defense Line of Amsterdam
1997 Mill Network at Kinderdijk-Elshout
1997 Historic Area of Willemstad, Inner City, and Harbour, the Netherlands Antilles
1998 Ir.D.F. Woudagemaal (D.F. Wouda Steam Pumping Station)
1999 Droogmakerij de Beemster (Beemster Polder)

NEW ZEALAND
1990 Tongariro National Park
1990 Te Wahipounamu – South West New Zealand*
1998 New Zealand Sub-Antarctic Islands
* Westland/Mount Cook National Park and Fiordland National Park, previously inscribed on the World Heritage List, are part of this site.

NIGER
1991 Air and Ténéré Natural Reserves
1996 W National Park of Niger

NIGERIA
1999 Sukur Cultural Landscape

NORWAY
1979 Urnes Stave Church
1979 Bryggen
1980 Røros
1985 Rock Drawings of Alta

OMAN
1987 Bahla Fort
1988 Archaeological sites of Bat, Al-Khutm and Al-Ayn
1994 Arabian Oryx Sanctuary

PAKISTAN
1980 Archaeological Ruins at Moenjodaro
1980 Taxila
1980 Buddhist Ruins at Takht-i-Bahi and Neighboring City Remains at Sahr-i-Bahlol
1981 Historic Monuments of Thatta
1981 Fort and Shalamar Gardens in Lahore
1997 Rohtas Fort

PANAMA
1980 Fortifications on the Caribbean side of Panama: Portobelo-San Lorenzo
1981 Darien National Park
1997 The Historic District of Panamá, with the Salón Bolivar

PARAGUAY
1993 Jesuit Missions of La Santisima Trinidad de Parana and Jesus de Tavarangue

PERU
1983 City of Cuzco
1983 Historic Sanctuary of Machu Picchu
1985 Chavin (Archaeological site)
1985 Huascaran National Park
1986 Chan Chan Archaeological Zone
1987 Manu National Park
1988 Historic Centre of Lima
1990 Rio Abiseo National Park
1994 Lines and Geoglyphs of Nasca and Pampas de Jumana

PHILIPPINES
1993 Tubbataha Reef Marine Park
1993 Baroque Churches of the Philippines
1995 Rice Terraces of the Philippine Cordilleras
1999 Historic Town of Vigan
1999 Puerto-Princesa Subterranean River National Park

POLAND
1978 Cracow's Historic Centre
1978 Wieliczka Salt Mine
1979 Auschwitz Concentration Camp
1980 Historic Centre of Warsaw
1992 Old City of Zamosc
1997 The Medieval Town of Torun
1997 Castle of the Teutonic Order in Malbork
1999 Kalwaria Zebrzydowska the Mannerist architectural and park landscape complex and pilgrimage park

PORTUGAL
1983 Central Zone of the Town of Angra do Heroismo in the Azores
1983 Monastery of the Hieronymites and Tower of Belem in Lisbon
1983 Monastery of Batalha
1983 Convent of Christ in Tomar
1988 Historic Centre of Evora
1989 Monastery of Alcobaça
1995 Cultural Landscape of Sintra
1996 Historic Centre of Oporto
1998 Prehistoric Rock-Art Sites in the Côa Valley
1999 Laurisilva of Madeira

REPUBLIC OF KOREA
1995 Sokkuram Buddhist Grotto
1995 Haeinsa Temple Changgyong P'ango, the Depositories for the Tripitaka Koreana Woodblocks
1995 Chongmyo Shrine
1997 Ch'angdokkung Palace Complex
1997 Hwasong Fortress

ROMANIA
1991 Danube Delta
1993 The Villages with Fortified Churches in Transylvania
1993 Monastery of Horezu
1993 Churches of Moldavia
1999 Historic Centre of Sighisoara
1999 Dacian Fortresses of the Orastie Mountains
1999 Wooden Churches of Maramures

RUSSIAN FEDERATION
1990 Historic Centre of St. Petersburg and Related Groups of Monuments
1990 Kizhi Pogost
1990 Kremlin and Red Square, Moscow
1992 Historic Monuments of Novgorod and Surroundings
1992 Cultural and Historic Ensemble of the Solovetsky Islands
1992 White Monuments of Vladimir and Suzdal
1993 Architectural Ensemble of the Trinity Sergius Lavra in Sergiev Posad
1994 Church of the Ascension, Kolomenskoye
1995 Virgin Komi Forests
1996 Lake Baikal
1996 Volcanoes of Kamchatka
1998 Golden Mountains of Altai
1999 Western Caucasus

SAINT CHRISTOPHER & NEVIS
1999 Brimstone Hill Fortress National Park

SENEGAL
1978 Island of Gorée
1981 Djoudj National Bird Sanctuary
1981 Niokolo-Koba National Park

SEYCHELLES
1982 Aldabra Atoll
1983 Vallée de Mai Nature Reserve

SLOVAKIA
1993 Vlkolinec
1993 Banska Stiavnica
1993 Spissky Hrad and its Associated Cultural Monuments

SLOVENIA
1988 Skocjan Caves

SOLOMON ISLANDS
1998 East Rennell

SOUTH AFRICA
1999 Greater St. Lucia Wetland Park
1999 Robben Island
1999 Fossil Hominid Sites of Sterkfontein, Swartkrans, Kromdraai and Environs

SPAIN
1984 Historic Centre of Cordoba
1984 Alhambra, Generalife and Albayzin, Granada
1984 Burgos Cathedral
1984 Monastery and site of the Escurial, Madrid
1984 Parque Güell, Palacio Güell and Casa Mila in Barcelona
1985 Altamira Cave
1985 Old Town of Segovia and its Aqueduct
1985 Monuments of Oviedo and the Kingdom of the Asturias
1985 Santiago de Compostela (Old town)
1985 Old Town of Avila, with its Extra-Muros churches
1986 Mudejar Architecture of Teruel
1986 Historic City of Toledo
1986 Garajonay National Park
1986 Old Town of Caceres
1987 Cathedral, Alcazar and Archivo de Indias in Seville
1988 Old City of Salamanca
1991 Poblet Monastery

1993 Archaeological Ensemble of Mérida
1993 Royal Monastery of Santa Maria de Guadalupe
1993 Route of Santiago de Compostela
1994 Doñana National Park
1996 Historic Walled Town of Cuenca
1996 La Lonja de la Seda de Valencia
1997 Las Médulas
1997 The Palau de la Música Catalana and the Hospital de Sant Pau, Barcelona
1997 San Millán Yuso and Suso Monasteries
1998 University and Historic Precinct of Alcalá de Henares
1998 Rock-Art of the Mediterranean Basin on the Iberian Peninsula
1999 Ibiza, Biodiversity and Culture
1999 San Cristóbal de La Laguna

SRI LANKA
1982 Sacred City of Anuradhapura
1982 Ancient City of Polonnaruva
1982 Ancient City of Sigiriya
1988 Sinharaja Forest Reserve
1988 Sacred City of Kandy
1988 Old Town of Galle and its Fortifications
1991 Golden Temple of Dambulla

SWEDEN
1991 Royal Domain of Drottningholm
1993 Birka and Hovgården
1993 Engelsberg Ironworks
1994 Rock Carvings in Tanum
1994 Skogskyrkogården
1995 Hanseatic Town of Visby
1996 Church Village of Gammelstad, Luleå
1996 The Laponian Area
1998 Naval Port of Karlskrona

SWITZERLAND
1983 Convent of St. Gall
1983 Benedictine Convent of St. John at Müstair
1983 Old City of Berne

SYRIAN ARAB REPUBLIC
1979 Ancient City of Damascus
1980 Ancient City of Bosra
1980 Site of Palmyra
1986 Ancient City of Aleppo

THAILAND
1991 Historic Town of Sukhothai and Associated Historic Towns
1991 Historic City of Ayutthaya and Associated Historic Towns
1991 Thungyai-Huai Kha Khaeng Wildlife Sanctuaries
1992 Ban Chiang Archaeological Site

TUNISIA
1979 Amphitheater of El Jem
1979 Site of Carthage
1979 Medina of Tunis
1980 Ichkeul National Park
1985 Punic Town of Kerkuane and its Necropolis
1988 Medina of Sousse
1988 Kairouan
1997 Dougga/Thugga

TURKEY
1985 Historic Areas of Istanbul
1985 Göreme National Park and the Rock Sites of Cappadocia
1985 Great Mosque and Hospital of Divrigi
1986 Hattusha
1987 Nemrut Dag
1988 Xanthos-Letoon
1988 Hierapolis-Pamukkale
1994 City of Safranbolu
1998 Archaeological Site of Troy

TURKMENISTAN
1999 State Historical and Cultural Park "Ancient Merv"

UGANDA
1994 Bwindi Impenetrable National Park
1994 Rwenzori Mountains National Park

UKRAINE
1990 Kiev Saint-Sophia Cathedral and Related Monastic Buildings, Kiev-Pechersk Lavra
1998 L'viv – the Ensemble of the Historic Centre

UNITED KINGDOM
1986 Giant's Causeway and Causeway Coast
1986 Durham Castle and Cathedral
1986 Ironbridge Gorge
1986 Studley Royal Park, including the Ruins of Fountains Abbey
1986 Stonehenge, Avebury and Associated Sites
1986 Castles and Town Walls of King Edward in Gwynedd
1986 St. Kilda

1987 Blenheim Palace
1987 City of Bath
1987 Hadrian's Wall
1987 Westminster Palace, Westminster Abbey and Saint Margaret's Church
1988 Henderson Island
1988 Tower of London
1988 Canterbury Cathedral, St. Augustine's Abbey and St. Martin's Church
1995 Old and New Towns of Edinburgh
1995 Gough Island Wildlife Reserve
1997 Maritime Greenwich
1999 The Heart of Neolithic Orkney

UNITED REPUBLIC OF TANZANIA
1979 Ngorongoro Conservation Area
1981 Ruins of Kilwa Kisiwani and Ruins of Songo Mnara
1981 Serengeti National Park
1982 Selous Game Reserve
1987 Kilimanjaro National Park

UNITED STATES OF AMERICA
1978 Mesa Verde
1978 Yellowstone
1979 Grand Canyon National Park
1979 Everglades National Park
1979 Independence Hall
1980 Redwood National Park
1981 Mammoth Cave National Park
1981 Olympic National Park
1982 Cahokia Mounds State Historic Site
1983 Great Smoky Mountains National Park
1983 La Fortaleza and San Juan Historic Site in Puerto Rico
1984 The Statue of Liberty
1984 Yosemite National Park
1987 Monticello, and University of Virginia in Charlottesville
1987 Chaco Culture National Historic Park
1987 Hawaii Volcanoes National Park
1992 Pueblo de Taos
1995 Carlsbad Caverns National Park

URUGUAY
1995 Historic Quarter of the City of Colonia del Sacramento

UZBEKISTAN
1990 Itchan Kala
1993 Historic Centre of Bukhara

VENEZUELA
1993 Coro and its Port
1994 Canaima National Park

VIETNAM
1993 Complex of Hué Monuments
1994 Ha Long Bay
1999 Hoi An Ancient Town
1999 My Son Sanctuary

YEMEN
1982 Old Walled City of Shibam
1986 Old City of Sana'a
1993 Historic Town of Zabid

YUGOSLAVIA
1979 Natural and Culturo-Historical Region of Kotor
1979 Stari Ras and Sopocani
1980 Durmitor National Park
1986 Studenica Monastery

ZAMBIA/ZIMBABWE
1989 Mosi-oa-Tunya/Victoria Falls

ZIMBABWE
1984 Mana Pools National Park, Sapi and Chewore Safari Areas
1986 Great Zimbabwe National Monument
1986 Khami Ruins National Monument

Literaturhinweise

Zum Verzeichnis der gesamten Graz Literatur siehe:
For an index of complete Graz literature see:

Österreichische Kunsttopographie (bearbeitet von Wiltraud Resch),
Die Kunstdenkmäler der Stadt Graz, Die Profanbauten des I. Bezirkes, Bd. LIII, Wien 1997.

Graz – Stadtarchitektur – Architekturstadt; Architektur und Stadtentwicklung 1986–1997,
(Hg. Amt für Stadtentwicklung und Stadterhaltung, Magistrat Graz), Graz 1997.

Wiltraud Resch, Attila Mudrák,
Die Stadtkrone von Graz, Graz-New York, 1994.

Kubinzky Karl A. und Astrid M. Wentner,
Grazer Straßennamen, Herkunft und Bedeutung, Graz 1998.

Lebensraum mit Geschichte – Der Grazer Schloßberg,
Hg. Karl Adlbauer und Thomas Ster, Graz 1998.

Historische Jahrbücher der Stadt Graz
(Stadt Graz, Hg. F. Bouvier und H. Valentinitsch (Red.), Graz 1968-1999.